Panoramic view of the rolling hills of Ellicott City looking north toward the courthouse. Emory Methodist Episcopal Church is on the right and "Capitoline Hill" is on the left, circa mid 1800s.

ELLICOTT CITY VOLUNTEER FIREMAN'S ASSOCIATION

INCORPORATED

1927

MARYLAND

REMEMBRANCES
OF PASSING DAYS
A PICTORIAL HISTORY OF ELLICOTT CITY AND ITS FIRE DEPARTMENT

CAROLE ANN ZINK

BY B. H. SHIPLEY JR.
AS TOLD TO WILLIAM K. KLINGAMAN, Ph.D.

The Donning Company/Publishers
184 Business Park Drive, Suite 106
Virginia Beach, Virginia 23462

Steve Mull, General Manager
B. L. Walton Jr., Project Director
Dawn V. Kofroth, Assistant General Manager
Mary Jo Kurten, Associate Editor
Chris Decker, Art Director/Graphic Designer
Tony Lillis, Director of Marketing
Teri S. Arnold, Marketing Coordinator

Library of Congress Cataloging-in-Publication Data

Shipley, B. H.
        Remembrances of passing days : a history of Ellicott City and its fire department / by B. H. Shipley, Jr. as told to William F. Klingaman.
        p.   cm.
Includes index.
ISBN 1-57864-004-0 (hardcover : alk. paper)
1. Ellicott City (Md.) Fire Dept.—Histpry. 2. Ellicott City (Md.)—
Social life and customs. I. Klingaman, William F. II. Title.
TH9505.E49071S53 1997
363.37'09752'81—dc21   97-27512

        CIP

Printed in the United States of America

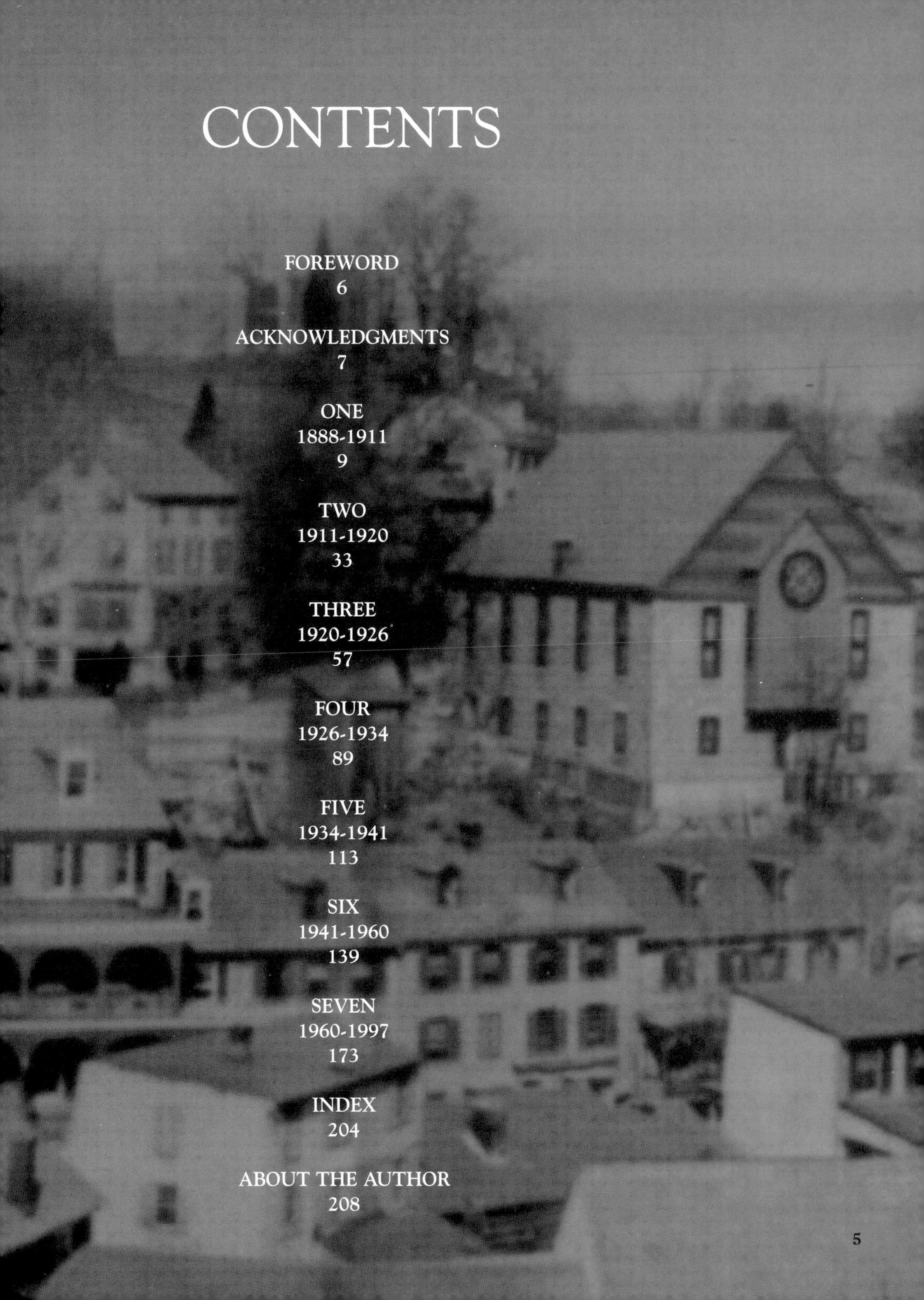

CONTENTS

FOREWORD
6

ACKNOWLEDGMENTS
7

ONE
1888-1911
9

TWO
1911-1920
33

THREE
1920-1926
57

FOUR
1926-1934
89

FIVE
1934-1941
113

SIX
1941-1960
139

SEVEN
1960-1997
173

INDEX
204

ABOUT THE AUTHOR
208

FOREWORD

In the natural course of human events, a community has to rely on its members for their common good. This book is a factual account of one such community—Ellicott City, Maryland—and the service provided to this community over the years by a group of dedicated men and women. It depicts the hardships and rewards experienced in protecting the area from the danger of fire and in recovering from major natural disasters. The Ellicott City Volunteer Firemen's Association motto is **"Service —Anywhere—Anytime."** This book is about those people.

H. Gregory Tornatore
Board of Directors, 1997

ACKNOWLEDGMENTS

FROM B. H. SHIPLEY JR.

Information and photographs were gathered from many sources. Without the help and cooperation of these people and organizations, this publication would not have been possible.

The Babe Ruth Museum

The Baltimore Streetcar Museum

The Baltimore Sun

Russell H. Baugher

Anne A. Beatty

The Catonsville Argus

Dr. Charles B. Clark

William P. Corun

Ellicott City Mayor and Town Council Minutes

The Ellicott City Times

Dale A. Gardner

Howard County Board of County Commissioners Minutes

Howard County Historical Society

The Howard County Times

William L. LeConte

Maryland Room–Enoch Pratt Free Library

Joseph P. Morea

E. Russell Moxley

Nora Novosad

St. Paul's Catholic Church

Carole Ann Zink

I am indebted to Carolyn S. Klein who performed a multitude of tasks.

FROM WILLIAM F. KLINGAMAN

It has been a pleasure to work on this project, combining the rich history of Ellicott City with the accomplishments of the brave men and women of the Ellicott City Volunteer Firemen's Association. This story could not have been told, however, without the contributions of B. H. Shipley Jr. and Carolyn Klein. Over the decades, Mr. Shipley has maintained an irreplaceable treasure of historical documents relating to the history of the town and its firefighters. These documents, along with Mr. Shipley's own recollections, form the basis of this history. Mrs. Klein was responsible for organizing this history project, researching the historical files, copyediting the manuscript, and generally coordinating the entire effort. I would like to take this opportunity to thank both Mr. Shipley and Mrs. Klein for their assistance, for they completed the lion's share of the work on this volume.

1774 - Patapsco Flouring Mills - 1906
Ellicott City, Maryland -
Daily Capacity 2000 Barrels   C. A. Grambrill Mfg. Co. Prop.

ONE
1888-1911

In the summer of 1888, the United States was in the midst of one of the most tumultuous decades of economic and technological growth in the nation's history. Progress was the watchword for Americans, as machinery and electricity transformed the pace and scope of American life, revolutionizing both the workplace and the home with such inventions as Alexander Graham Bell's telephone, Thomas Edison's incandescent light bulb, and George Pullman's luxurious railroad cars. Industrial giants such as Andrew Carnegie and John D. Rockefeller were amassing huge fortunes. Record numbers of immigrants poured into cities such as New York, Philadelphia, and Chicago, straining the resources of local governments. And the society columns of newspapers were filled with the scandals and lavish parties of Vanderbilts

and Astors. In Maryland, economic development continued apace as the state enjoyed the prosperity derived from the burgeoning trade at the port of Baltimore. If the pace of life seemed a bit slower in rural Howard County, the summer of 1888 still represented an important step forward for Ellicott City. That was the year that witnessed the establishment of the first organized fire-fighting company—known as Volunteer Fire Company No. 1—in the history of the town. Ellicott City already had been incorporated for twenty-one years by the time the city's first fire company was formed, though the town still lacked electrical power, public transportation, or any comprehensive public water system. There was, however, a newly founded telephone company whose offices were located over the James H. Gaither Livery Stable (8267 Main

Street). Concern over potential damage to life and property from fires had been a frequent concern during the years following incorporation, and the City Council had approved numerous resolutions concerning the need for fire protection. Judging from the minutes of t he Council, the local government's primary anxiety about fires clearly had been the failure of some residents to adequately maintain the condition of their chimneys.

On June 9, 1867, the Council approved an ordinance mandating residents to clean their chimneys and flues twice a year. If a local inspector discovered that any chimney was in disrepair, he had the authority to condemn it and order the homeowner to make the necessary repairs. Seven years later, the Council added a provision that ordered all newly built chimneys and flues to be made of brick or stone, obviously in response to the fire hazards presented by more flammable materials. Still, the local property owners seemed to have neglected the proper maintenance of their chimneys.

In the autumn of 1878, Ellicott City's sole policeman reported that he had found it necessary to have sixty-six chimneys cleaned. The following year, the Council authorized the mayor to hire "a responsible person" to clean the chimneys of negligent residents. In some ways, it was a thankless job. Within a month, the mayor had hired Mr. Frank M. Shipley to handle the job, but when Shipley subsequently presented the Council with a bill for his services, he was told to collect the money from the property owners himself.

Mr. Shipley appeared to have found the requirements of his job somewhat onerous, for he resigned shortly afterward. Less than two years later the Council again dispatched written warnings ordering all residents whose chimneys needed repair to immediately have the work done. This time the Council asked Mayor Charles J. Werner to purchase whatever tools were necessary to clean the city's chimneys, and to obtain advice from the Baltimore City government about the best method of ensuring that all the chimneys would be properly maintained. To save time and money, Werner decided to use the stock of hickory brooms which the police officer had already bought. In an attempt to put the weight of law enforcement behind their motions, the Council then directed the city's policeman to hire a chimney sweeper (who would receive 50 percent of all fees derived from his work) and stringently enforce the law covering the cleaning of chimneys and the collection of fees from recalcitrant property owners.

In those days, whenever a fire broke out, the bell at a local church was rung to alert the citizenry. Everyone who was able to respond would grab a bucket or ladder to form a "bucket brigade" and help quench the blaze. By 1888, however, the Council had decided that such informal, ad hoc methods of fire protection were no longer sufficient. Since Ellicott City needed an organized fire-fighting force, Volunteer Fire Company No. 1 was formed July 10, 1888.

A membership roster of the Company from the first year consisted of thirty-five individuals, all of whom paid annual dues to support the work of the Company. It reveals that representatives of many of the town's most prominent families participated in the work of the Company right from the start, including Christian Eckert, proprietor of the Howard House Hotel who was elected mayor in 1890, William F. Mayfield, Benjamin Mellor, Justice B. H. Wallenhorst (who doubled as a haberdasher), and the town's leading dentist, Dr. M. Gist Sykes. Membership in the Volunteer Fire Company was open to all males above eighteen years of age and who were "of good moral character." Once the Company was formed, new members were elected by a ballot of the existing membership. All members were expected to obey all of the orders given by the Company's chief

marshal and his assistants, to attend regular meetings of the company, and to seek to increase the Company's efficiency. Anyone found guilty of insulting one of the officers or taking any action that might impugn the integrity of the Company would be expelled.

During that first summer, meetings were held frequently—eight meetings in the first six weeks—at the town hall (8044–8046 Main Street) to elect officers and organize the work of the Company. Owen H. Mericer, a local businessman who lived on the hill near the county courthouse, served as the Company's first president. He was assisted by Vice President B. H. Wallenhorst, Secretary Frank Heine, the station manager for the Baltimore & Ohio Railroad, and Treasurer Dr. M. Gist Sykes. The Company also elected a Board of Directors who were responsible for maintaining the truck house and the Company's equipment, and to loan out any of the Company's apparatus in an emergency. For its first chief marshal, the Company elected W. T. McCauley. As chief marshal, McCauley had—in the words of the Company's bylaws —"entire charge of the apparatuses when called into service," including the authority to direct the members of the Company during firefighting emergencies to "prevent the wanton destruction of property which so often occurs at fires." Chief

First Fire House 1889–1923.

Benjamin Mellor's carriage depositary, circa 1875.

McCauley was assisted by Deputy Marshals Frank Heine and L. J. Kinsel, both of whom had responsibility for supervising the formation of bucket lines, and assuming the duties of the chief marshal in his absence.

On August 24, the Company voted to authorize the purchase of a hand-drawn ladder truck, complete with leather buckets, for $550 from the Charles T. Holloway Company of Baltimore City. The truck was subsequently put into service October 5, 1888. The next step was to obtain a building to house the truck. At first, the Company planned to construct a two-story structure. After encountering difficulty in raising the necessary funds (an estimated $800), the Board of Directors decided to settle for a more modest one-story house at 511 Ellicott Street (3829 Church Road), on a triangle lot donated by Christian Eckert. Civic-minded residents helped keep the cost of construction down by contributing their labor—carpentry, painting, and putting on the tin roof—at no charge. The truck house was completed in the late spring of 1889.

To help pay off its remaining start-up debts and defray its operating expenses, the Company decided to hold a five-day bazaar in February 1890. This tradition would later be revived and last for more than half a century. The first event, held at the firehouse and the second-floor hall of Benjamin Mellor's Carriage Depository (vacant lot, 3826 Church Road), proved a rousing success. Numerous items were raffled off, including jewelry, ornaments, clocks, and barrels of flour contributed by well-wishers. Nearly eighty couples came out from Baltimore City on a special train to attend the ball held on Wednesday night at the New Assembly Room. After 1910, this Assembly Room was converted to four frame row houses, (8548–8560 Frederick Road.) By the time the festivities had ended, the Company had raised the impressive total of $290.

Within days, however, the Volunteer Fire Company faced its first major test. Several fires broke out at Maupin's University School, a private school located on Columbia Avenue (3976 Old Columbia Pike). On March 3, 1890, the school suffered extensive damage from a fire. Subsequent events led investigators to determine that the blaze may not have been an accident. Several days after the initial fire, smoke was seen pouring from the attic of a

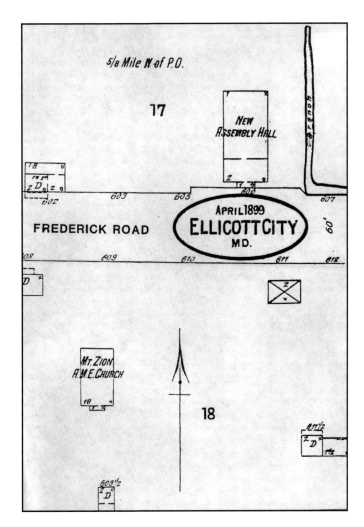

New Assembly Room used for public meetings and social events, circa 1885.

storeroom at the school. Fire company investigators discovered that the fire had been deliberately set in wooden barrels filled with flammable rubbish and paper. Yet another alarm was sounded that same day, and again the Company managed to quell the fire with only minor damage.

Damage caused by arson was not limited to Ellicott City itself in those days. In November 1890, a series of fires on farms just outside the town led the Howard County Commissioners to offer a reward for the apprehension and con-

Ellicott City 1907 street scene looking west (8055 Main Street).

9:00 P.M. Saturday, October 3, 1891, while the streets of the town were filled with shoppers and partygoers, a coal oil lamp in an upper story of the Enterprise No. 1 Dry Goods & Notions Store on lower Main Street started a blaze. It eventually encompassed the adjacent establishment, another dry goods store owned by Justice B. H. Wallenhorst. The fire spread so rapidly and burned so fiercely that for a time it seemed that the entire street might go up in flames.

Town officials telegraphed to Baltimore City for help and dispatched an urgent telephone message to the Catonsville Fire Company in nearby Baltimore County, across the Patapsco River. Fortunately, the Catonsville company had a chemical engine that brought the blaze under control. The Baltimore City Fire Department had already loaded an engine on a special B & O train bound for Ellicott City before they received word their assistance would not be needed. When the debris had cooled, the damage to the Enterprise store, owned by James J. Lamkin, was estimated at $1,200, while Mr. Wallenhorst's establishment suf-

viction of the person responsible for setting fire to a hay barrack on the farm of Elias Blackshire. Similar fires of suspicious origin had been set in the same area on other farms, destroying stocks of fodder and fencing materials.

Since the county was still predominantly rural in the late nineteenth century, summertime brought the danger of field fires, particularly in the dry summer and autumn months. Barns frequently burned, with the attendant loss of wheat, hay, and farming implements. Farms that lay next to a railroad track faced a special hazard. Sparks from passing locomotives occasionally started fires that destroyed crops or nearby woods.

But the most serious fires in the Ellicott City area remained those that occurred in the more heavily populated areas of the town. Many of the town fires were caused by spills from oil lamps or heat from wood or coal stoves. At fered losses of approximately $600. Mayor Edward Norris subsequently sent special written thanks to the chiefs of both the Catonsville and Baltimore City fire departments, as well as the superintendent of the B & O Railroad, for their willingness to help the town during the crisis.

Several years later, an arsonist set fire to the historic mansion known as "White Hall." One of the earliest dwellings in Howard County, it was the former home of Judge Richard H. Ridgely and Colonel Charles W. Dorsey. At the time of the blaze in the late winter of 1893, White Hall was owned by Mrs. Mary T. Ligon. Shortly before midnight March 14, someone set fire to two outside doors of the house. The caretaker of the mansion and his family barely escaped with their lives by lowering themselves by a sheet from a window and then dropping to the ground before the flames consumed the house.

Reconstruction of the house was completed in 1901. Approximately forty acres of the original estate and the residence are now listed in the National Register of Historic Places.

Later in 1893, a fire broke out in the engine room of a sewing establishment in the building known as the town hall (8044–8046 Main Street) which was also occupied by a printing firm, the Patapsco Lodge, several families, and a dispensary. A gasoline engine in the sewing room caught fire on the evening of November 23, 1893. The flames soon threatened to demolish the entire building. For two hours the Fire Company battled the blaze, trying to keep it from spreading into the main part of the building. After considerable effort they managed to quench the fire. Although the room suffered considerable damage, the rest of the town hall was spared.

Not all the Fire Company's calls were quite so dramatic. On a warm July evening in the summer of 1892, the Company responded to a report of a fire at the home of a family living on Court House Lane, behind Talbott & Clark's Lumberyard. Around ten o'clock that night, with most of the town's residents already asleep, someone had noticed smoke emanating from the house. With anxieties heightened by a recent rash of fire scares, the alarm was sounded before anyone took the time to investigate. The Fire Company rushed to the scene and crashed through the front door of the dwelling. "The crash was followed," according to one contemporary report, "by tramping feet and wild-eyed men who looked like giants and who seemed to wield axes and all sorts of horrible weapons. . . . The street was full of hubbub as though a regiment were outside.

"Howe" hand-operated, horse-drawn pumper.

As Volunteer Fire Company No. 1 became an established institution in Ellicott City, it continually sought to upgrade the quality of its firefighting equipment. Following the success of the initial bazaar, the Company decided to make the event an annual occasion. In the early years, the bazaar frequently was held at Benjamin Mellor's Carriage Depository. Sufficient funds were raised to enable the Company to purchase a six-gallon shell fire extinguisher, new lamps and fixtures for the truck, rods to hold the buckets on the truck, and a sixteen-foot scaling ladder.

But the pride of the Company was both the two-wheeled hose cart and a Howe "Side Stroke" hand-operated, horse-drawn piston pumper. The hose cart was known as "the Jumper," because it could easily be jumped over curbs. The pumper was purchased and placed in service in December 1894. It was known as "Squirrel Tail" for the suction hose which curved back over the rig when it was not in use. The pumper cost the City $1,050. Before the Mayor and City Council committed to purchasing the engine, however, they insisted on putting it through a series of tests to prove its efficiency.

On Tuesday evening, December 4, a huge crowd of townspeople turned out to observe the bright red, highly pol-

Then came a rattle of wheels, the clank of metal, and the tumult of voices without. The horrible cry of 'FIRE' and the ringing of fire bells greeted the occupants of the house, who were completely taken aback by the appearance of the firemen." As it turned out, the smoke had come from a cooking stove which the family traditionally placed on their rear porch during the hot summer months. The lady of the house had only been baking a pie for the family's lunch the following day. Although the Fire Company presumably apologized for the intrusion, the family waited several days for the city authorities to repair their front door.

ished engine at work. The engine was designed to be operated by manpower, with horizontal bars along the length of the vehicle. These were

An 1894 two-wheeled hand-drawn hose cart. On display in the Firehouse Museum—3829 Church Road, Ellicott City, Maryland.

manipulated by six to eight men. As the bar on one side was raised, the bar on the other side descended, thereby producing the power for the pump. In the test demonstration, the engine produced a stream of water that shot into the air thirty feet higher than the five-story town hall building. Members of the Volunteer Fire Company were able to land streams of water on the roof of the town hall with ease. The engine also proved capable of drafting water vertically nearly 30 feet through the suction hose, then forcing it over a 200-foot elevation through 350 feet of hose before sending the water in a horizontal stream toward a blaze.

As part of the test, the engine was then taken to Granite Hill (Oella Avenue), where it used a chemical mixture of soda, acid, and water, and then a stream of water pumped from the nearby Patapsco River to extinguish a sixteen-foot frame building that had deliberately been set ablaze. The town authorities were so impressed by this

performance that they agreed on the spot to purchase the engine. It was a popular decision, for the pumper was subsequently named by the *Ellicott City Times* as "one of the best investments ever made by our city."

The Company decided to obtain a fire alarm bell. (There appeared to be a general consensus that the bell and alarms the Company had been using were far too small to serve as an adequate warning.) In an attempt to save

Baltimore & Ohio Railroad locomotive bell.

*J. Regester & Son
"Big Bell."*

money, the Company accepted in March 1894 a ninety-pound bell and yoke that the Baltimore and Ohio Railroad offered free of charge. This bell, too, proved inadequate, because its limited carrying range meant that it could not be heard in all parts of the town. (It was later employed as a school bell at the Ellicott City Elementary and High School, subsequently served the congregation of St. Luke's AME Church at 8411 Frederick Road, and is currently located in the Firehouse Museum at 3829 Church Road. Consequently, the Company launched a search for another new bell, one with a deeper tone and a wider range that would sound an alarm different from all other bells in Ellicott City. The city finally purchased a suitable bell crafted by the Baltimore firm of J. Regester & Son, and placed it into service July 4, 1896. Placed in the cupola of the engine house, the booming

tones of "Big Bell," as it came to be known, reached all sections of the town, indicating the location of a fire by the number of strokes it sounded.

By this time, the Company had grown to more than seventy-five members. Owen H. Mericer still served as president, but the post of vice president had been assumed by Benjamin Mellor, assisted by Secretary Robert C. Wilson and veteran Treasurer Dr. M. Gist Sykes. Following the death of Chief Marshal W. T. McCauley, Mr. Bradley T. Scaggs had been appointed to direct the efforts of the Company.

In the closing years of the nineteenth century, a series of serious fires tested the efficacy of the Fire Company's new officers and equipment. On the evening of Sunday, June 12, 1898, a group of buildings on the farm of William Manly, about a mile and a half northeast of Ellicott City, caught fire. The conflagration grew quickly, until the flames were clearly visible from the hilltops around the town. Thinking quickly, a local businessman named James H. Gaither, the proprietor of a livery stable on Main Street (U. S. Post Office, 8267 Main Street), who had just arrived for evening church services in a horse-drawn carriage, unhitched his horses and attached them to the fire engine. A contingent from the Volunteer Fire Company then assumed control, driving the engine down Main Street, which by this time was crowded with curiosity-seekers. When the firefighters arrived at the Manly estate, they found a group of citizens attempting to fight the flames without noticeable success. With the help of the Catonsville Fire Company, the firefighters of Company No. 1 managed to save most of Manly's property.

Just one day later, the residents of Ellicott City heard the fire bell ringing again. This time, the blaze was located in town, in the office of Frank Heine, the ticket agent of the B & O Railroad.

Semi-convertible trolley with rope fender—route between Saratoga Street, Baltimore City, and Ellicott City, circa 1900.

Although the Company managed to bring the fire under control fairly quickly, a considerable quantity of valuable documents were lost. Subsequent investigations revealed that the fire had been deliberately set by three young men from Howard County, one of whom confessed to the crime and implicated his accomplices.

Less than a month later, the town suffered yet another fire, when the Thomas H. Hunt Livery Stable (8098 Main Street), suffered heavy damage. The stable caught fire on the morning of July 4, while more than a thousand Ellicott City residents were celebrating at a picnic on the grounds of the United Railway & Electric Company

Main Street looking west. On the left side of the street is one of the Oldfield's originial long-handled wooden pumps (8133 Main Street).

(Miller's Bottom, off Westchester Avenue), the trolley company that had inaugurated service to the town earlier that year. Suddenly they heard the cry of fire. Someone had been exploding fireworks on Main Street, when the fragment of an exploded firecracker struck the shingle roof of Hunt's stable. As soon as the crowd realized what was happening, they rushed to the scene. The Fire Company managed to limit the damage to the stable, but the incident demonstrated just how easily a devastating fire might strike the Main Street area.

During the first decade of the twentieth century, town authorities began to investigate more sophisticated methods of providing fire protection for Ellicott City. In June 1900, James H. Gaither offered to install ten fire hydrants along the streets of the city so the fire company could cover the entire business and residential area with its existing equipment. At that time, Gaither's open concrete reservoir (seventy feet long, forty feet wide, and nine feet deep) was the source of the only public water system—the Ellicott City Water Works—in the town. It filled from springheads on a hillside (Ellicott Mills Drive and Fel's Lane). "That was the public water," noted former Fire Department Chief B. H. Shipley Jr., "and it just wasn't adequate and reliable for fire protection. Over the years, it became inadequate for other uses, even though Mr. Gaither extended the line out to what we call Sucker Branch (Our Lady Center, 3301 Rogers Avenue) in 1909, to draw water into the reservoir."

All that lay in the future. Contemplating Gaither's proposal to install fire hydrants along Main Street, the *Ellicott City Times* noted that the plan would provide "a sense of security against a wholesale destruction of the town by fire never before enjoyed by our citizens." Further, the newspaper's editors predicted that insurance rates would decrease if the project were approved. Nevertheless, Gaither's plan encountered severe resistance within the City Council. The Council rejected the plan initially, and then reconsidered it in the spring of 1902. During a meeting on May 6, 1902, Gaither again offered to install ten fire hydrants at an annual rental cost of twenty-five dollars per fire hydrant. Again the Council decided against spending funds for the project. As one councilman explained, "I don't see the necessity of these hydrants unless we can use them to sprinkle the streets."

In years to come, the question of procuring an adequate water supply to enable the Fire Company to fight fires effectively would continue to cause considerable controversy. For the time being, only one fire hydrant was installed on Main Street in the autumn of 1902, on a parcel of land at the corner of Main and Forrest Streets owned by Ms. Rebecca Talbott, the sister of lumberyard owner E. Alexander Talbott. That corner also marked the end point of the six-inch water main that extended down Main Street from the Ellicott City Water Works reservoir (Ellicott Mills Drive and Fel's Lane). Inquiries revealed that fire hydrants were given the nickname of "Fire Plugs" in the early 1800s in New York City. The water mains were bored-out logs with large wooden plugs. The plugs could be removed so water would be available for the fire engines to use.

Another successful enterprise was begun by James H. Gaither. His horse-drawn wagons had previously picked up packages from the Catonsville terminus of the City & Suburban Railway and delivered them to Ellicott City. Edward D. "Uncle Ed" Hilton, a prominent member of the Volunteer Fire Company No. 1, drove teams of horses working for Mr. Gaither. On May 29, 1900, the Gaither City & Suburban Express Company was incorporated to provide electric rail service between Ellicott City and Baltimore. Shipments included ice by the ton, dressed hogs, lumber, barrels of whiskey, barrels of flour and cement. Freight cars and power were provided by the United Railway; the Gaither City & Suburban Express Company provided the rest of the operation. Many passengers complained about delays when the freight cars often stopped to load and unload cargo. The appearance of motorized trucks made business decline. Operations ceased December 31, 1912.

While the City Council debated the expense of upgrading the town's fire-fighting capabilities, a series of blazes—which investigators insisted were deliberately set—struck the Weber Stone Quarries, located along the Baltimore & Ohio Railroad tracks, about a quarter of a mile below Maryland Avenue. The first fire burned an engine house at the quarry; the second, in mid-November 1901, destroyed the quarry's stone

For many years the Gaither's City and Suburban Express Trolley operated over the No. 9 line between Ellicott City and Baltimore City. After the Express Service was discontinued December 31, 1912, the trolley was used by the maintenance way department.

Main Street looking west from Kraft's Meat Market (8081 Main Street), circa 1900.

crusher and several other buildings, while ruining additional expensive machinery and causing losses of nearly $20,000.

In June 1905, the Fire Company decided to turn over all of its property to the city. Two years later, in November 1907, the title to the Fire Company equipment, funds, and property passed to local authorities. To oversee the maintenance of the firehouse and its apparatus, the Ellicott City government subsequently appointed a Committee of Public Safety, consisting of three of the town's most prominent citizens: Samuel J. Yates, William F. Kirkwood, and John Reichenbecker. Three years later, the city had to consider whether it wished to purchase the Ellicott City Water Works, when the assets of the water company were auctioned in March 1908. At the time, the Ellicott City Water Works property included Gaither's reservoir, along with more than ten thousand feet of water mains. Mayor Joseph H. Leishear Jr. called a public meeting at the Howard House—the town's leading hotel, founded in 1850 by Christian Eckert and his wife—to obtain public reaction to the proposed purchase of the water company. According to a contemporary news report, the taxpayers voted by a

High speed semi-convert-
ible trolley with rope
fender—route between
Baltimore City and
Ellicott City, circa 1905.

Trolley trestle bridge, cov-
ered wooden bridge, and
Radcliffe's Emporium.
(8000 Main Street)

2-1 majority to approve the purchase. Nevertheless, after an engineer inspected the works, which apparently were not in perfect condition, the City Council decided not to make any bid on the property. Instead, the company was purchased by one of James H. Gaither's sons, who was expected to restore the waterworks to better working condition.

Two potentially disastrous fires in the main part of Ellicott City over the next two years made it clear that the town would need additional firefighting equipment. On the afternoon of March 17, 1908, a fire broke out in the Cumberland and Cullen Paint Shop, located on the second floor of Lilly's Bottling House (8217 Main Street), next to the telephone exchange on Main Street. The shop was vacant at the time. If there had been any significant breeze to fan the flames, the fire probably would have gotten out of control, demolishing the Lilly building and the adjoining structures. Fortunately, a telephone operator smelled smoke and sounded an alarm, enabling a bucket brigade to extinguish the blaze before it caused serious damage.

Then, on the afternoon of December 2, after nearly all the employees at the county courthouse had gone home for the day, the deputy clerk, Martin Batson, discovered smoke billowing

James H. Gaither's livery stable, and above it on the second floor, the Citizens Telephone Company of Maryland Exchange.

from the treasurer's office. Clerk Batson at once gave the alarm, and many of the male citizens of the town turned out to help the Fire Company fight the flames. Nevertheless, virtually everything in the treasurer's office was completely destroyed. Once again, the absence of any wind helped limit the damage to a single office, but the county had come very close to losing all of its irreplaceable records.

The following month, the City Council moved to upgrade the town's firefighting apparatus by purchasing a case of fire extinguishers and three hundred feet of fire hose. This reopened once again the issue of installing fire hydrants to help protect the city. The Council began investigating the purchase of another, more modern fire engine. As it deliberated, the city suffered yet another fire, this time in the main equipment room of the Maryland Telephone Company Exchange, located on the second floor of the James H. Gaither's Livery Stable. (At that time, Ellicott City had two telephone companies: the Citizens Telephone Company of Maryland, owned by Maryland Telephone Company Exchange; and the Howard Telephone Company, a branch of C & P Telephone Company, whose switchboard was located over Dr. Isaac J. Martin's Drug Store.)

Shortly before midnight January 10, 1910, during a heavy snowstorm, an electrical fire broke out at the Citizens Telephone Company of Maryland. Miss Bessie Holtman, the operator on duty, realized the danger at once and ran out into the street shouting, "Fire!" When no one appeared to respond to her screams, the eighteen-year-old Miss Holtman ran through the snow to the fire engine house, broke open the back door, and made her way to the fire alarm bell and pulled the rope for all she was worth. Within minutes volunteers from the Fire Company appeared, and managed to use the hand-pumper truck—whose hose they attached to a recently installed fire hydrant at the corner of Main Street and Forrest

Street—to send a stream of water into the office, dousing the flames. As a token of the appreciation of the city's business community, the Board of Trade presented the unflappable Miss Holtman with fifty dollars in gold, plus a medal in recognition of her services. The fire marked the end of the Citizens Telephone Company, however. After the fire, the company sold its lines and telephones to the C & P Telephone Company.

Not surprisingly, the City Council soon invited a representative of the Howe Engine Company to make a presentation explaining the merits of the various new models of fire engines the company had to offer. To help raise the requisite funds for a new engine, the Council sought help from local property owners and the Howard County Commissioners. Within six months, sufficient funds had been raised to permit the Council to purchase a Howe "Barode" horse-drawn triplex pumper with a gasoline operated pump. The new engine, which cost $2,000 (less a $400 trade-in allowance for the old Howe "Side Stroke" hand-operated pumper), was placed into service at the Ellicott Street fire station July 10, 1910. It had a gasoline operated pump with the capacity of 250 gallons of water per minute, and reportedly could throw streams of water from Main Street all the way over the courthouse, and from the Patapsco River at the Baltimore & Ohio Depot over the buildings of Rock Hill College. Unfortunately, the engine had one major drawback: it was extremely difficult to start and proved somewhat undependable.

In fact, it was said that only one man in Ellicott City—Charles A. Herrmann, an insurance broker and member of the City Council who had long been interested in firefighting, and who served as the engineer of the Fire Company—could start and operate the engine with any degree of regularity. "Consequently," noted one veteran member of the Fire Company, with perhaps only a slight touch of exaggeration, "when we had a fire, Mr. Herrmann had

to be on hand or the fire just burned." Moreover, events would demonstrate that it often took the horse-drawn engine between thirty and ninety minutes to reach fires outside the immediate Main Street area. This delay allowed numerous fires to rage out of control before the firefighters arrived.

Ellicott City's purchase of a new fire engine was only one indication that the town really was entering the twentieth century. During the period from 1890 to 1920, the United States witnessed an explosion in the number of public high schools in cities and towns across the nation. Before that time, most localities had only provided free education through the sixth or, at most, the eighth grade. Students then had to attend private academies before continuing their education at the university level, or obtain vocational training on their own. The combination of labor reform laws—which prohibited the use of child labor—and the influx of immigrants from southern and eastern Europe (who allegedly needed to be "Americanized")

Ellicott City Elementary and High School. Note the Fire Department's 1894 bell on loan, mounted on the vestibule roof. This building was razed in 1933 by local contractor Henry House & Sons. Photo circa 1920.

26

at the turn of the century fueled the drive to provide public education at the high school level, and over each decade in the early twentieth century, the number of public high schools in the United States doubled.

Ellicott City—and Howard County—obtained its first public high school in 1902 (class of 1906), when several rooms were added to the grammar schoolhouse that had stood on School Street (3673 Park Avenue) since 1889. Before that time, the town's children had been educated at three different schools: a small building called Hill Street School that served as an elementary school (8508 Hill Street); the venerable Friends' School at the Quaker meeting house on Quaker Hill (3771 Old Columbia Pike); and the basement of the German Evangelical Lutheran Church (3761 Church Road). In 1889, Ellicott City's school commissioners approved the construction of the four-room school on Park Avenue; in 1904, a manual training department was added. Then, with funding assistance from the Board of County School Commissioners, the town built two additional large recitation rooms which provided sufficient space for what was known as a "Standard High School."

At that time, Howard County had approximately one thousand students at all grade levels combined, and spent

$32,000 a year on education. The curriculum at the high school level included the usual classical studies of French, German, Latin, English literature, and ancient history, but local authorities were proud to note that their new high school would also offer courses in agriculture and dietetics. The former subject seemed particularly appropriate, since 80 percent of all of the county's students were expected to make their living from agriculture. "It is vastly more important," noted Colonel William S. Powell, the editor of the

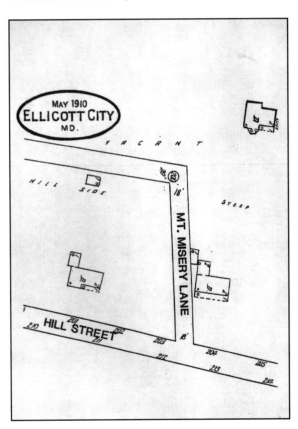

Mount Misery Lane (off 8467 Hill Street)—main access to John F. Kirkwood's home—upper right. The entrance is now 8453 Frederick Road. Mr. Kirkwood had a private water system for his use and several neighbors supplied from springs on the hillside along Cat Rock's Stream. He was proprietor of Kirkwood's Footwear Store (8129 Main Street).

Ellicott City Times, at the dedication ceremony of the Ellicott City Elementary and High School November 9, 1906, "that you should learn how to make two blades of grass to grow where one grows now, and how to carry on this great business of agriculture which means the feeding of all the people of the world with the least amount of labor and the greatest amount of profits to yourselves."

Hill Street Primary Grade School, circa 1885.

Governor Edwin Warfield also spoke at the dedication ceremony, extolling the educational opportunities that existed for Ellicott City's children—far greater, he insisted, than the opportunities he had been offered in his own childhood. At the end of the ceremony, Professor Thomas Gladden, the principal of the school, received the keys to the new rooms. Principal Gladden, however, was the only male involved in

the town's educational system. His assistant principal and the school's three teachers were all women.

In the early years of Ellicott City High School, students sometimes had to adapt to unusual circumstances. The high school's first graduating class had to hold its commencement at the Howard County Courthouse. The first class to have a yearbook was the class of 1915, which held its graduation in the Oppenheim Oberdorf & Company Shirt Factory, located on Fel's Lane (Parking Lot F).

Despite the evidence of increasing sophistication and growth—by 1907, for instance, the town had more than 150 telephones and played host to scores of vacationers from Baltimore City each

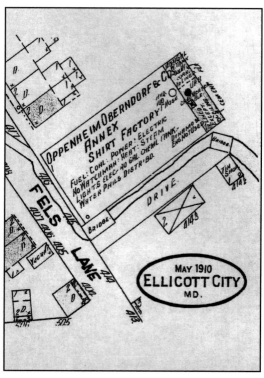

The class of 1915 held graduation in the Oppenheim Oberdorf & Company Shirt Factory.

summer—Ellicott City remained very much a rural town in many ways, dominated by the male members of the community. Gatherings of the local courts were almost entirely male-dominated affairs.

One such occasion, which nearly turned out to be disastrous for the town, took place December 29, 1908, when more than 150 members of the community assembled at the second-floor hall of Easton Son's Blacksmithing and Wheelrighting (a vacant lot at 3826 Church Road) to observe the indictment of a man accused of assaulting and robbing a white resident of Howard County. The alleged assault had occurred December 15 when a well-known county farmer, Charles E. Hill, had been attacked and robbed in the area known as Paradise, a section of Catonsville. A Baltimore County policeman investigating the incident had arrested a black man named William Hatwood for the crime, and subsequently turned him over to the Ellicott City authorities.

On the afternoon of December 29, a preliminary hearing was held at Eastons Son's Hall, which often served the county as a courtroom. By the time the hearing began at 2:30 P.M., there were nearly 150 people inside the hall—some of them armed—trying to get a glimpse of Hatwood. More were outside trying to push their way into the courtroom.

Shortly after the trial magistrate, Justice B. H. Wallenhorst, began the proceedings, the floor of the courtroom buckled and broke beneath the weight of the crowd, sending scores of people tumbling down onto the concrete floor fifteen feet below. Broken pieces of timbers, furniture, and beams pinned the bodies to the ground, while others panicked and began a stampede over the wounded. Hatwood, too, was caught beneath a heavy block of wood. Those who had hoped to lynch him found themselves thwarted by the accident.

An unofficial account of the incident listed fifty townspeople—all of them men—with serious injuries, including Judge Wallenhorst (who was taken to the hospital with internal injuries), Sheriff George W. Howard,

Easton Son's Hall collapses. The dotted lines show how the floor fell.

Fire hydrant and coupling wrench.

State's Attorney Martin F. Burke, and Ellicott City Police Chief Julius Wosch. To avoid further trouble, Sheriff Howard instructed several deputy sheriffs to put the handcuffed Hatwood in a carriage, with a deputy on either side of him, and take him to the terminus of the trolley line at Main Street and Fel's Lane. There a waiting car—with instructions not to stop—sped through Ellicott City and took the accused man to the Baltimore City jail, where he remained until his trial.

After the town recovered from the shock of this incident, Ellicott City continued to modernize its firefighting equipment and water facilities. To supplement the new "Howe" engine it had purchased in 1910, the City Council decided, in a unanimous vote, to authorize the Ellicott City Water Works to place five fire hydrants at strategic locations along Main Street: in front of J. H. Kramer's Salon (8055 Main Street); in front of Altra Caplan's Dry Goods Store (8125 Main Street); in front of Steward's Grocery Store (Main Street and Columbia Avenue); at the corner of Main Street and Forrest Street; and in front of the Charles T. Makinson residence (across from 8401 Frederick Road). The fire hydrants were installed by the first week of May 1911. A special brass hydrant wrench was needed to operate these fire hydrants. One opening in the wrench was pentagon-shaped and was used to open the valve and remove the caps. Another opening in the wrench, a three-quarter-inch square, was used to open the valve to the steamer connection. A third opening, shaped like a circle, was used for pin type hose couplings.

Still, the public water system served only a very limited section of the town. Many Ellicott City residents needed to rely on private sources of water, including hand pumps located along Main Street (8046, 8129, 8202, and 8357 Main Street); Frederick Road (8433 Frederick Road) and St. Paul Street (3760 St. Paul Street) and two additional pumps located on Columbia Avenue (3774 and 3815 Old Columbia Pike). Even these were not sufficient to serve the town's needs, however. In the late winter of 1911, the city suffered one of the most spectacular fires in its history.

The General Merchandise Store owned by Edward B. and Mary A. (Koeder) McDonald, 6 Oella Avenue. The McDonalds raised six children in the upper floors of the building and ran a restaurant and bar on the ground level until Prohibition. It became a confectionery and dry goods store until 1948. It later housed the Valley Inn and is currently the Trolley Stop Restaurant. The building dates back to the early 1800s.

The Patapsco Hotel. Over the years it had various names. At one time it was an ice plant (8006–8026 Main Street). Note the covered walkway over the Tiber Branch and the covered stairway to the railroad station, circa early 1900s.

TWO
1911-1920

On the afternoon of March 16, 1911, Dr. F. X. McKenny, the president of St. Charles College—a Catholic seminary located on Frederick Turnpike about five miles west of Ellicott City (Terra Maria, in the 10800 block of Frederick Road)—was standing in front of the college chapel when he smelled smoke. Originally built on land donated by Charles Carroll, the college had been a fixture in the Ellicott City area since it opened its doors in 1832; among its numerous notable graduates was the famous Baltimore prelate Cardinal Gibbons. It stood on one of the highest plateaus in Howard County and included a main building, made out of square-cut granite, nearly 370 feet in length, along with several dormitories and the lovely Gothic chapel, which reportedly was modeled after the famous church at Aix-la-Chapelle in France.

But the fire that broke out on that windy, bitterly cold March afternoon destroyed all of this beauty. Within thir-ty minutes from the time Dr. McKenny first noticed the smoke and discovered the fire raging in the chapel, most of the college was in flames. By the time the Fire Company arrived, there was little it could do to save any of the buildings. Fortunately, the students and nuns who lived in the wings of the main building managed to throw their belongings out of the windows, but the priests were less fortunate, having lost nearly everything they owned. Several hours later, as night fell, all that remained amid the devastation were crumbled ruins of stone walls, a piano resting on its side, books lying on the ground with their leaves loose and blowing in the wind, and framed pictures with shattered glass tossed against marble statues. Virtually all of the college's manuscripts and paintings had been destroyed, along with nearly twenty thousand volumes from the two libraries.

The covered wooden bridge over Patapsco River connecting Baltimore and Howard Counties, circa 1910.

When Philip Carroll, the heir to the Carroll estate, received news of the fire, he immediately opened Doughoregan Manor, the family mansion, to shelter the residents of the college. Battling the blaze in the bitterly cold temperatures had taken a toll on the firefighters as well. While attempting to put out the flames, Julius Wosch, Ellicott City's chief of police (in fact, the town's only regular policeman), who often joined the members of the Volunteer Fire Company in emergencies, had been completely soaked with water. Because it was so cold, he had neglected to remove his overcoat. By the time he returned home, he found that the water on his coat had frozen so hard he could not remove the garment. Finally he managed to crawl out of the frozen coat, and then stood it up on the floor of his office as a memento of the St. Charles College fire.

Although the trustees of St. Charles College attempted to launch a rebuilding campaign at once, so classes could begin again the following autumn, the diocese eventually decided to move the college to a more central location in Catonsville, where it would be more accessible to public transportation.

The St. Charles College fire was only the first of several disastrous fires

St. Charles College, cornerstone blessed July 11, 1831, opened as a college in the fall of 1848.

that plagued Ellicott City during the decade of 1910–1920. Shortly after midnight May 21, 1913, a conductor on the town's electric trolley line noticed flames shooting from the back of the Charles T. Makinson Carriage Factory at the corner of Main Street and Fel's Lane. After alerting Mr. Makinson, who lived nearby, the conductor ran down the street shouting an alarm. Within minutes the Fire Company reached the scene. Since the Makinson shop was extremely dry, the flames had spread to the adjoining building, a grocery store above which the family of Nimrod Johnson lived. A local man who had just returned to town from Baltimore City on the midnight train rushed into John-son's home and roused the sleeping family. He then carried three of the Johnson children to safety while Johnson and his wife saved their other two children.

Meanwhile, the Fire Company had managed to hook a section of hose to one of the recently installed fire hydrants. Along with the sometimes obstreperous fire engine—which decided to cooperate on this occasion—the Company had two streams of water to play upon the flames. The Catonsville fire engine arrived shortly after the alarm sounded. Even with the aid of their Baltimore County brethren, how-

ever, the firefighters needed the help of a bucket brigade formed by bystanders who had gathered to observe the conflagration.

An additional danger arose when several electrical wires from the Patapsco Light Company caught fire above the building, causing the electric company to cut off its current until the blaze was extinguished. Once again the absence of strong wind helped the firefighters bring the flames under control, but not before both buildings and nearly all of their contents were destroyed. Unfortunately, neither Makinson nor Johnson carried insurance on their buildings. In fact, Johnson's insurance policy had expired the previous week, and he had failed to renew it in time. Subsequently, the United Railway would purchase one part of the site of Makinson's blacksmith shop for use as a terminus for their trolley. (That portion of the Makinson lot is currently the parking lot adjoining the firehouse—8390 Main Street.) The remainder of the Makinson property remained vacant for two decades, until the town's new firehouse was built on the site in 1939.

A year later, one of Ellicott City's most historic structures vanished in flames when the wooden-covered bridge over the Patapsco River, connecting Baltimore and Howard counties, caught

Trolley No. 9 approaching Main Street—water flowing over Patapsco River Dam. Far left: W. B. Bennett's Rental Housing known as "Bennett's Row" (Parking lot A). This was the birthplace of the author, circa 1950.

Looking west from Westchester Avenue Bridge, No. 9 Trolley, known as "The Jerkwater," is entering "the cut," a rocky defile, and passing through heavy foliage.

Left: St. Paul's Rectory, St. Paul Street, built in the 1840s. Priest on the porch is Rev. Peter B. Tarro, D.D., a pastor at St. Paul's Catholic Church from 1883 to 1907.

fire and burned. The venerable white pine bridge, one of the few remaining structures of its kind in the state, had been erected in 1870 to replace the previous bridge, which had been swept away in the devastating flood of 1868. Although the structure had recently begun to sag, leading the local authorities to bolster it with an additional abutment in the center, it still provided a vital service to the community. It served farmers from Howard, Frederick, and Montgomery Counties, who transported their produce and livestock to Baltimore City markets via Frederick Road. The trolley used the reinforced

Covered wooden bridge over the Patapsco River— connecting Baltimore and Howard Counties—was destroyed by fire June 7, 1914.

United Railway's trestle that spanned the Patapsco River alongside the wooden structure.

The fire began Sunday afternoon, June 7, 1914, when an automobile crossing the bridge leaked gasoline from its tank. Another car, occupied by

young men smoking cigarettes, followed close behind. Apparently one of the occupants of the second car tossed a lighted cigarette out of a window. Passersby reported hearing a violent explosion followed at once by a burst of flames on the bridge. Both the Ellicott City Fire Company and the Catonsville engine responded to the alarm, but the Catonsville company's apparatus jammed. Meanwhile, the Ellicott City firefighters—seeing that the dry pine bridge could not be saved—decided to concentrate instead on preserving the United Railway bridge. Much to their dismay, however, the balky gasoline-powered pumper sputtered several times and then lapsed into silence. It took a Herculean effort from Engineer Charles A. Herrmann to rouse the engine back into activity. The fire company managed to run two lines of hose from the river. Although the railway trestle caught fire several times, the firemen quickly extinguished the flames each time.

Once again, electrical wires posed a hazard to the firefighters, as the wires along the bridge began to snap when the flames reached the top of the structure. When the first large wire fell on the car rails about a yard from the Ellicott City end of the bridge, there was a large explosion and a burst of white flame. This led the Fire Company to prudently withdraw to the safety of Radcliff's Coal yard (8000 Main Street, Parking Lot B) nearby, until the electric current could be turned off. In the end, the Baltimore County section of the wooden bridge burned completely and fell into the river. All that remained of the Howard County section were charred timbers and the forlorn stone abutments. The railway bridge was saved, however, and within an hour after the blaze had abated, trolley traffic resumed. Nevertheless, the loss of the wooden bridge proved a serious inconvenience to the county's farmers, who had to drive far out of their way, to either Ilchester or Hollofield, to cross the Patapsco and reach Baltimore City.

It was only the start of a string of disasters. One of the most devastating fires in the history of Ellicott City broke out the following winter, late on the evening of January 14, 1915. The blaze began in the grocery store operated by Marshall Bacon on the south side of Main Street, east of Columbia Avenue (8173–8197 Main Street). Just before eleven o'clock, Charles B. Wallenhorst—who owned a haberdashery just three doors up from the Bacon building—noticed smoke pouring from the grocery store, and immediately called the Fire Company to sound the alarm.

When the volunteers arrived, they quickly decided they could not cope alone with the conflagration, which already had consumed Bacon's Store and Souris's Candy Kitchen next door. A message immediately went to Catonsville for assistance. Together, the Ellicott City and Catonsville companies—aided by scores of residents who formed a series of bucket brigades—attempted to stem the blaze by pumping water from two fire hydrants and a nearby branch of the Patapsco, but the flames kept mounting higher and higher. Meanwhile, other volunteers rushed into the frame buildings in the path of the raging fire to waken and evacuate their sleeping residents.

At 11:45, a desperate call went out to the Baltimore City Fire Department, but the city refused to send any help, pointing out that all the available sources of water already were being used. "Our engines would have been of no use whatever," explained the chief engineer of the Baltimore City Fire Department. "We were anxious to do whatever we possibly could to help, [but] our apparatus would have been of absolutely no use."

As the candy store crumbled and Butke's General Store disappeared in flames, the fire continued to spread up Main Street to the Wallenhorst

Looking west from railroad bridge. Flooding caused by Tropical Storm Eloise September 1975.

Flooding at Main Street and Maryland Avenue caused by Tropical Storm Eloise September 1975. Note that water is almost up to the emergency telephone on the pole straight ahead.

Six-alarm fire (8143–8167 Main Street), November 14, 1984.

Six-alarm fire destroyed several businesses November 14, 1984.

Building, made of stone, and the three-story post office. At this point some of the townspeople began to panic, fearing the fire would spread to the block of buildings across the street. Realizing that the post office was almost certainly lost, several postal employees rushed into the building and brought out as much of the mail as they could, along with money orders and other valuable documents. For their part, the fire companies decided to focus their efforts on the buildings across the street, dousing their roofs with water to keep them from breaking into flames.

By 1:30 A.M., the fire finally had begun to subside, its progress broken by the efforts of the firefighters and the existence of a vacant lot on the other side of the post office. In the end, all five buildings were completely destroyed. Estimates of the total damage reached as high as $40,000, some of which was not covered by insurance. Most of the owners of the devastated structures swore they would rebuild in the wake of the holocaust, but for the time being they were forced to move their businesses and residences into temporary quarters. In 1920, the property that had housed the post office building was purchased by the La Salle Council of the Knights of Columbus, who planned to build a hall for their meetings there. The Knights never followed through on their plans, however, and the lot was subsequently sold to Isaac H. Taylor, who built a furniture and jewelry store on the site (8197 Main Street). Mr. Taylor and his family lived on the third floor of the building, above his store.

It could have been much worse, and the town authorities knew it. Several months earlier, Mayor John H. Kraft had called a public meeting to discuss the need for a more modern and efficient firefighting department, but almost no one responded. Now, however, there appeared a groundswell of support for the formation of a reorganized fire department. The *Ellicott City Times* encouraged the movement by printing an advertisement on its front page, urging citizens to attend a meeting called by the city commissioners to reorganize and revitalize the Volunteer Fire Company at once. "Do NOT wait to be urged," it declared. "You are as much interested as anyone. If you can't attend, SEND IN YOUR NAME."

Accordingly, a huge crowd appeared at the meeting at the fire engine house January 25. Clearly the townspeople now understood how much havoc a fire could wreak among the wooden frame buildings that lined Main Street. The fire also had demonstrated that an adequate supply of water—long a nemesis of Ellicott City firefighters—was absolutely essential to the town's fire protection efforts, as was an efficient and well-trained corps of firefighters. Indeed, the latter topic occupied most of the meeting that evening. "The old days," reported one observer, "when everybody did their best and not much was accomplished because of the lack of systematic effect seemed to be in the past, and now we are to have a firefighting force well organized, properly officered and with each active member having his duties mapped out before the fire starts."

As a model for the reorganized Ellicott City Fire Department, the president of the city commissioners, Mr. J. Edwin Kroh, held up the Junior Fire Department of Frederick, which had been organized in 1839. As part of President Kroh's proposal, members of the Fire Department would go through Ellicott City, requesting all residents, taxpayers, and businessmen to join the Department. Obviously not everyone could personally take part in the activities of the Department, but those who were not actively involved in firefighting would lend the Department their moral and, perhaps more importantly, financial support. A score of the town's most prominent citizens signed up to

join the company that night, including William F. Mayfield, Isaac H. Taylor, J. Booker Clark, Leonard A. McNabb, Dr. Benjamin Mellor Jr., Police Chief Julius Wosch, James H. Gaither Jr., Joshua and William Dorsey, George O. Mellor, and Frank and William Miller. Those who attended the meeting also elected officers for the reorganized Company: Dr. William B. Gambrill, president; Richard S. Feigley and J. Hartley Johnson, vice presidents; Dulany C. Higinbothom, secretary and Richard Talbott, son of the owner of Talbott's Lumberyard, treasurer.

Almost at once the active firefighters of the Company began to hold weekly meetings and drills. Every Wednesday night the volunteers went through a series of exercises designed to increase their knowledge of the equipment and its use. To build team spirit, the Company decided to form two baseball teams—one from the hook and ladder company, and another from the hose company. And to raise funds to purchase additional equipment, including rubber coats and boots, the Company sponsored a carnival, held on the courthouse lawn, on three evenings in June. A series of booths, illuminated by electric lights, offered a wide variety of food and crafts, including lemonade, ice cream, and cakes, but the most pop-

ELLICOTT CITY I
STAT

4150 MON
ELLICOTT

E DEPARTMENT
ON 2

ERY ROAD
MARYLAND

ular attraction appeared to be the gypsy tent, where a pair of pretty young women told their customers' fortunes for a nickel.

Meanwhile, the work of recovering from the devastating fire went on. To decrease the chances of another, even more damaging holocaust on Main Street, the Ellicott City Commissioners approved an ordinance requiring all new buildings within the city limits to be constructed of brick, stone, or some similarly nonflammable material. For their part, the business owners who had lost their properties in the fire had no intention of building their renovated structures with wood. Mr. Wallenhorst, for instance, settled on a three-story brick building for his haberdashery, as did Edward Malone, who owned the property on which Marshall Bacon had

operated his grocery business. In fact, Mr. Malone's new building also had a white sand brick front, firewalls, and a tin roof. It presented such an attractive appearance that the Chesapeake and Potomac Telephone Company agreed to rent it for ten years to house their offices.

Neither the City Commissioners' ordinance, nor the reorganization of the Fire Company, however, could prevent the outbreak of new fires in the Ellicott City area. In the early morning hours of November 28, 1915, another blaze broke out, this time in the lumber shed of the E. A. Talbott Lumber Company, located on Court Avenue. Fortunately, the crew of the late-night trolley spotted the flames. After summoning help from nearby residents, they used their switch rod to tear off burning shingles

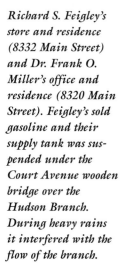

Richard S. Feigley's store and residence (8332 Main Street) and Dr. Frank O. Miller's office and residence (8320 Main Street). Feigley's sold gasoline and their supply tank was suspended under the Court Avenue wooden bridge over the Hudson Branch. During heavy rains it interfered with the flow of the branch.

from the top of the building. The flames were extinguished with only minor damage, but further investigation revealed a partially burned copy of the *Baltimore Sun* stuffed under the eaves of a lumber shed, leading authorities to conclude that the fire had been deliberately set.

When officials reviewed the records of recent fires, they also discovered that several other minor fires in the western section of town—which was then a mix of residences and businesses, including Talbott's Hardware Store (8308 Main Street) and Feigley's General Merchandise Shop (8332 Main Street)—had broken out at about the same time of night (between ten-thirty and midnight) over the past year. In fact, ten fires had occurred over the past eighteen months within a few hundred yards of the terminus of the trolley line (Main Street & Fel's Lane). The major fire that had consumed Charles T. Makinson's carriage establishment two years earlier had started within a stone's throw of the Talbott Lumberyard.

Their suspicions aroused, Ellicott City officials asked the state fire marshal to investigate the Talbott incident. Within a week, the fire marshal's office had arrested a forty-five-year-old motorman on the late-night trolley—popularly known as "the Owl"—and charged

Patapsco Flouring "Mill D" 1916 fire. On bridge over the Old Mill Race is Ellicott City's "Barode" pumper. To far right is Ellicott City's horse-drawn ladder wagon.

him with setting the fire on November 28. The motorman, George W. Ross, had been seen leaving his trolley on the night of the fire, walking down a lane toward the Talbott yard. A few minutes after he and the trolley departed, the blaze was discovered. Ross, who had formerly lived in Ellicott City, admitted that he set the Talbott fire to get even with Talbott. Apparently he had once rented a house from Talbott, and the two men had a disagreement about a stove that Ross had installed. Although the fire marshal's office suspected that Ross had been involved in other fires in and around Ellicott City, and in a number of minor fires around his home on Calverton Road, on the outskirts of Baltimore City, Ross refused to acknowledge any role in any incident other than the Talbott Lumberyard blaze.

Certainly Ross played no role in starting the fire that destroyed a large flour mill and warehouse at the Patapsco Flouring Mills—C. A. Gambrill Manufacturing Company on the north side of Frederick Road, just across the Patapsco River in Baltimore County, on the morning of April 19, 1916. The C. A. Gambrill Manufacturing Company, established in 1774 by Charles Carroll and a member of the Gambrill family, had long been one of the areas's leading flour and cornmeal suppliers. The company had built the six-story mill, known as "Mill D," in 1840, out of brick and sheet iron. In 1904, it had been remodeled, enlarged, and equipped with modernized machinery. Since the outbreak in 1914 of World War I—then termed "the Great War"—the mill had been operating virtually around the clock to fill orders from the governments of Great Britain and France. In fact, it had just finished an order for 125,000 barrels of flour for the Allies, and investigators suggested that the friction of constantly running machinery in the mill might have provided the initial spark for the fire.

The fire was spotted around five o'clock in the morning. Within minutes, the Ellicott City Fire Department was at the scene, having hauled its engine down Main Street and across the river. The Catonsville engine had already arrived. The two companies realized right away that with the flames pouring out of the roof of the mill, there was no chance of saving it—even with a dozen streams of water playing on the structure—or the grain elevator, where twenty thousand bushels of wheat were stored, waiting to be milled. Instead, they tried to save the plant's other buildings, including the office, the packing department, and the original mill (built in 1809 with bricks imported from England by the Ellicott family). Although sparks frequently fell on the adjoining structures—including the plant of the Electric Company about half a mile away—the fire companies managed to extinguish all the minor fires before they could cause any significant damage. Mill D and the warehouse, however, were almost completely destroyed, at a loss estimated at $200,000. All that remained were the charred ruins of the mill's red brick walls. Recognizing that the walls were

Ruins of Patapsco Flouring "Mill D" after 1916 fire.

48

so unstable that they represented a danger to anyone working near the site, the Ellicott City Fire Company dynamited them to the ground. The fire turned out to be a significant, albeit temporary, blow to the area's economy. More than sixty residents of Ellicott City who were employees of the mill found themselves temporarily out of work, because the remaining buildings could produce nothing but cornmeal. Further, numerous Howard County farmers had counted on selling their grain to the C. A. Gambrill Company for milling. Fortunately, the demands of the war in Europe had created myriad economic opportunities for enterprising entrepreneurs, and other firms managed to pick up the slack while C. A. Gambrill Company rebuilt its plant.

Within months C. A. Gambrill Company had erected a concrete mill and equipped it with modern machinery. Following the entry of the United States into the war in April 1917, the C. A. Gambrill Company had obtained a steady stream of government orders for flour and cornmeal. It was in the process of filling one of those orders in May 1918 when another fire erupted at the plant, this time in the only remaining original building. The fire broke out around 8:30 on the evening of May 18, and once again the Ellicott City Fire Company and its "Howe" engine—

Patapsco Flouring "Mill A," known as the "Old Mill," prior to the 1918 fire.

which decided to cooperate splendidly on this occasion—arrived on the scene shortly after the motorized Catonsville engine. They were followed closely by firefighters from the nearby communities of Mount Washington, Mount Winans, and Arlington. Inside the burning building were two hundred barrels of lard, two carloads of soda, one thousand barrels of flour, one hundred tons of sugar, ten thousand bushels of corn, two hundred and fifty barrels of cornmeal, and a thousand bushels of oats. Not surprisingly, the age of the building, combined with the stores of grain and lard, rendered the fire inextinguishable. Once again, the fire companies focused their efforts on saving the surrounding buildings, especially the new concrete mill.

By 9:30 the fire companies had managed to control the blaze, though it continued to smolder until one o'clock the following morning. The original building was a complete loss. The railroad trestle over the Patapsco River, which had connected the plant with the Baltimore and Ohio Railroad tracks in Ellicott City, also had been wrecked. Although the fire affected fewer buildings than the devastating blaze two years earlier, the company once again suffered a significant financial blow, estimated at approximately $250,000.

Suspicions about the cause of the fire centered on the watchman, who was a gentleman of German extraction. At the time, this suspicion did not seem unusual. Once the United States had entered the war on the side of the Allies in April 1917, anxiety about the loyalty of German-Americans (or even Irish-Americans with a grudge against Great Britain) led many otherwise rational citizens to adopt "patriotic" measures that might have seemed somewhat exaggerated in retrospect. (It was during these years, for instance, that sauerkraut was renamed "liberty cabbage," and hamburger became "Salisbury steak," to avoid using German terms.)

The town's suspicions were fueled by the fact that the same watchman had been employed by another local company heavily engaged in filling wartime orders that had also suffered severe losses from a devastating fire. On the evening of January 25, 1918, a fire broke out at Dickey's Mills in Oella. The mill, which dated from 1815, had originally been engaged in the manufacture of cotton goods. It had been purchased in 1896 by William J. Dickey, who transformed it into a woolen mill. It had become so successful that it employed five hundred workers, many of whom lived nearby in housing owned by the company. In early 1918, the mill had been working on extra shifts to fill government contracts for army uniforms and blankets.

Because the mill was engaged in work for the government, company officials had assigned extra watchmen to ensure that no enemy aliens attempted to sabotage the plant. Nevertheless, a blaze erupted suddenly at the Oella plant in a room where loose raw wool, grease, and oil were stored. The coincidence of the same watchman being employed by both the C. A. Gambrill and the Oella mills seemed too much for many townspeople. As one longtime Ellicott City resident noted several decades later, "We were sure it was sabotage—but we could never prove it."

When the bell rang at the Ellicott City fire engine house that evening, the officers of the Fire Company paused briefly to consider their options. Since they had only an engine that had to be either horse-drawn or towed by truck, they decided not to attempt to haul it over a mile of hilly, slick winter roads to attempt to put out a fire that was already raging. Under the circumstances, the chances of actually making any significant contribution to quelling the fire seemed negligible. Nevertheless, several members of the Fire Department, along with scores of townspeople, headed for Oella to render whatever assistance they could.

The Fire Department's decision proved prudent. Although the Catonsville engine was able to keep the blaze away from the workers' houses, a fire engine from Baltimore City that had responded to the alarm found no other supply of water available—the minimal quantity of water in the mill race proved of little value—and simply turned around and returned to the city at once. Probably no combination of local firefighting forces could have stopped this fire in any case. The mill buildings were so full of highly combustible materials that the flames could be seen a mile away, and the intense heat from the blaze could be felt on the other side of the Patapsco River bridge, in Ellicott City. The firefighters did manage to save a large quantity of raw materials, and the bridge which connected the mill with the B & O Railroad remained intact. But the mill itself suffered over $250,000 damage, and its five hundred employees found

themselves temporarily out of work.

Ellicott City's firefighters made a far greater contribution in quelling another wartime blaze that occurred during the early morning hours of April 9, 1917. The fire appears to have started in Loughran's Bakery (8161 Main Street), located on the south side of Main Street east of Columbia Avenue. Joseph Kerger, who lived across the street, awoke shortly after midnight and noticed a red glow coming from the store on the other side. Once he realized what was happening, he sent his son to ring the bell at the fire engine house and ran to the bakery himself to awaken the owner, John Loughran. A contemporary observer noted that the firefighters arrived at the scene rapidly and set up their engine on Stewart's Bridge (at Main Street and Columbia Avenue). Calls also went out to Catonsville and Arlington. The Catonsville engine took up its position on Feigley's Bridge (Main Street and

Main Street in front of Patapsco Pharmacy (8090 Main Street), circa 1918.

Court Avenue), while the Arlington pumper set up on the banks of the Patapsco River.

Each engine employed two hose lines, but even with six streams of water playing on the blaze, the flames continued to spread. In a short time it had consumed the home of Catherine Reichenbecker and continued on to the home and pharmacy of Dr. J. Hartley Johnson, who was then vacationing in Atlantic City. On the other side of the bakery, the fire spread to Abraham Isaac's Clothing Store and then ignited the back of Charles Frey's Furniture and Hardware Store. In those days, many of the merchants of Ellicott City lived above their stores. Fortunately, everyone who was home asleep in these buildings managed to escape without serious injury.

By 4:30, the coordinated efforts of the fire departments had managed to put out the fires. The bakery had been completely destroyed, including recently purchased machinery and fifteen hundred loaves of bread. Mrs. Reichenbecker's home, too, was ruined, along with her household goods and furniture. The furniture in Frey's store suffered significant damage, but the building itself remained standing (8141–8167 Main Street).

No other major fires struck Ellicott City until the summer of 1920, but then a rash of fires set in motion a series of events that ended with the town's purchase of its first truly modern firefighting equipment. On the morning of July 2, 1920, a fire broke out at "Elk-Ridge" Farm mansion, the elegant home of J. Booker Clark and his family. The mansion, located on Cherry Lane (4200 block of Montgomery Road, the site of the Long Gate Shopping Center), was only seven years old, but it already had become well known as one of the most impressive homes in Howard County, with an estimated value of $250,000. The blaze appeared to have started in the third story of the Clark home. Even though the Ellicott City Fire Department responded quickly to the call for help by hitching the fire engine to the back of a truck, their efforts were thwarted by a familiar nemesis—the shortage of available water. In fact, there was an elevated concrete water tank on the Clark property, but due to a

Richard S. Feigley's warehouse and stable—Court Avenue (opposite Parking Lot E).

large crack in the structure, the tank was empty on that summer morning. (The tank was removed in 1996 for construction of the Target store in the Long Gate Center.) Although Mr. Clark and his family managed to save most of the furniture, fixtures, and clothing from their home, the mansion itself was gutted.

Less than two weeks later, another blaze broke out in Taylor Ridgeley's antiquated stable at the corner of Columbia Road and Main Street in Ellicott City. Since the fire started late on a Sunday morning, the sound of the fire bell interrupted the worship services in several local churches. A few ministers abruptly concluded their sermons to permit their congregations to help bring the fire under control. Within half an hour, the Volunteer Fire Company had quelled the flames. By the time the Catonsville engine arrived, the emergency was over.

Then, in the autumn of 1920, a series of four fires struck the Ellicott City area within the space of one week. On September 17, the barn of former sheriff Joseph Hunt, who lived several miles outside of town, caught fire— apparently from a match thrown into a pile of straw—while Hunt's workers were threshing wheat. Although the Ellicott City Fire Company arrived as soon as it could, neither the wheat nor the barn could be saved. "We are deeply grateful for the Ellicott City engine which did such excellent work, especially in coming so far up here," noted Hunt, but the lack of a motorized fire engine had once again cost the town dearly.

Less than a week later, a large barn on the property of the Summit Park Company in Catonsville—the former summer home of General James A. Gary, just a few miles up Frederick Road from Ellicott City—burned to the ground. At one point, the flames reached so high that residents of Ellicott City, looking eastward, thought they were witnessing another major fire in Baltimore City. The following morning, another barn fire occurred at "The Cedars," a Howard County farm belonging to Caleb D. Rogers. The prompt arrival of the Ellicott City Fire Company, which employed its chemical engine to battle the blaze, managed to save the other outbuildings on the Rogers farm, but equipment valued at nearly five thousand dollars was destroyed.

The final fire of this week of destruction struck the home of Albert Schatz of Columbia, the small town— really not much more than a post office and a general store—at the intersection of Columbia Road (Route 29) and Clarksville Pike (Route 108), just south of the Ellicott City line. Apparently the Fire Company's engine could not get to the scene in time, but volunteers managed to contain the fire by forming a bucket brigade, keeping the flames away from the nearby General Store and Columbia Post Office and the home of Henry E. Bloom. Although most of the Schatz family's possessions were saved, the house was almost completely destroyed.

Some observers believed that the occurrence of three barn fires in one week was no coincidence, and that the fires must have been deliberately set. Whether an incendiary was at work or not, however, the damage wrought by these fires, along with the devastating losses suffered by the C. A. Gambrill and Dickey mills during the war, persuaded the town authorities—and a host of local businessmen—that they needed to upgrade Ellicott City's fire protection equipment. Accordingly, City Commissioner Milton H. Easton launched a drive to obtain a motorized fire engine for the town. According to Commissioner Easton, numerous residents already had expressed their willingness to contribute toward the purchase of a more effective firefighting engine. "In the last couple of weeks," declared Commissioner Easton, "I have talked with a great many people relative to the need of a modern fire department for this town and community. The need for the improvement will not be questioned by anyone who realizes the great value of time when a fire alarm is sounded."

As Commissioner Easton pointed out, it took the town's present firefighting apparatus anywhere from thirty to ninety minutes to arrive at the scene of a fire. "If we had a motorized outfit," he predicted, "we could be on the scene of the fire up to a distance of five miles within a few minutes." Commissioner Easton also noted that the lack of an adequate water supply in the rural areas outside of Ellicott City also hampered firefighting efforts. "However," he added, "with modern equipment we could have probably gotten to the J. Booker Clark fire in time to save the buildings by the use of chemicals."

Commissioner Easton's claims for the speed with which a motorized fire engine could respond to alarms might have been too optimistic. In the early 1920s, the condition of the roads in Howard County left a great deal to be desired. Many of the county's main thoroughfares—Cherry Lane (later renamed Montgomery Road), Waterloo Road, and Route 175, for instance—were still largely dirt roads which frequently became impassable because they turned to mud in rainy weather. Columbia Road (Route 29) was paved from Ellicott City to Columbia. From that point to the intersection with Route 216 it, too, was nothing but dirt, as was much of Clarksville Pike

"Elk-Ridge" Farm concrete water storage tank, circa 1919.

(Route 108).

Within Ellicott City, Main Street was paved with cobblestones, split by the two sets of trolley tracks that ran from the trestle bridge across the Patapsco River up the hill to the intersection of Main Street and Fel's Lane. Here the cars were switched from one set of tracks to the other for the return trip to Baltimore City. There was also a second switch at the bottom of the hill, by Maryland Avenue, so the cars could return to Baltimore City without going up the hill in bad weather. Although only the wealthier residents of Ellicott City owned automobiles in the early 1920s, there still were occasional traffic jams with cars and wagons coming out of Maryland Avenue. The combination of narrow streets and the rutted trolley tracks posed a potential for traffic accidents, as the town soon learned to its sorrow.

Rock Hill College (3100 College Avenue).

THREE
1920-1926

Throughout the autumn of 1920, the movement to purchase a motorized fire engine continued to gain momentum. Commissioner Easton and the other leaders of the movement decided to try to obtain a substantial portion of the requisite funds from the residents who lived within an eight-mile radius of Ellicott City, by reminding them that a small contribution toward new fire equipment would easily offset the potential losses from the sort of fires that had recently plagued Howard County. "Farmers needed to realize," said Commissioner Easton, "that the engine and volunteer firefighters would be at their place in a few minutes from the time the alarm was sounded, and not only might be able to save many buildings after a fire has a start, but the chemicals will be an assurance against the loss of adjoining buildings."

To encourage support for the fire engine drive, the *Ellicott City Times* published an editorial reminding its readers of the damage already wreaked by fires that year. "Many thousands of dollars have been lost by men within a few miles of Ellicott City this summer as a result of fires," the newspaper noted, "and in several instances a great part of the property could have been saved had there been ample fire protection, amply equipped to reach the scene of disaster in time to begin work. "Perhaps the present horse-drawn engine could serve the needs of Main Street and the immediate area," the editorial continued, "but it certainly could not adequately protect the surrounding countryside." Support of this movement by men who own property will more than pay any taxpayer," it argued, "and the original cost will be the largest. Get behind it! Talk it up!

Pledge yourself and then get the other fellow to do the same."

The summer of 1920 had also brought vivid proof of the inadequacy of the Ellicott City public water system. For much of the spring and summer, two of the town's three pumps were broken, leaving only one pump working to provide water to the town. When that pump, too, failed at the end of July, the entire town was left without water for a whole week, save for a very slight stream that could be drawn in the lower elevations. An outraged citizenry complained vigorously to the owner of the waterworks, Mr. Robert Biggs, who promised to make the necessary repairs. In the meantime, town officials drew up a bill authorizing the city to increase its bonded indebtedness to allow it to install its own waterworks plant.

Meanwhile, the movement to obtain a motorized fire engine gained momentum. To provide a graphic illustration of the benefits of a motorized engine, the Howe Fire Apparatus Company—the manufacturer of the town's previous two engines—staged several demonstrations of its new equipment in early October. To emphasize the advantages of speed in an emergency, the Howe Company's engine drove from the firehouse to the sites of several recent fires, including the

Gambill Manufacturing Company and the ruins of the "Elk-Ridge" Farm mansion. Having witnessed the demonstration, veteran firefighter Charles A. Herrmann, one of the few men capable of working the Fire Company's present equipment, urged the community to support the drive for a new engine. "With homes and commercial buildings more difficult to find and more costly to build than ever before," said Mr. Herrmann, "too great stress cannot be laid upon intelligent individual precaution against fire." The rapid inflation and consumer shortages which followed the end of the war had made fire losses and the replacement of existing structures a burden on any business. "With the present scarcity of merchandise and the lack of sufficient labor, the destruction of goods by fire is a wicked waste," added Firefighter Herrmann. "The movement for new fire equipment deserves the earnest, vigilant support of every man, woman and child in Howard County."

But the traditional reluctance of the town and county governments to fund new projects forced the drive for motorized firefighting equipment onto a back burner. It would take more than staged displays and logical arguments to move the Ellicott City Commissioners to action. In the meantime, the outlying areas around the town continued to suffer serious losses from fire. In January 1921, the "Sixteen-Mile House," an eighteenth-century tavern that had become an historical landmark, burned to the ground. The tavern, located on the Frederick Pike near Mayfield, reportedly had once played host to General George Washington and several of his officers during the Revolutionary War. It also had served as the meeting place for Democratic Party gatherings and barbecues in Howard County, as the site of numerous horseracing contests, and as a stopping place for travelers heading from Baltimore City to the west. Apparently a defective chimney flue started the fire. The historic structure and virtually all of its contents were destroyed before the Fire Company arrived.

Several weeks later, another of Howard County's finest dwellings "Dalton Farm," the home of J. Lawrence Clark in Columbia (Dalton Community)—was destroyed by fire. Originally constructed with brick imported from Europe, Dalton Farm had stood for more than a century a few miles outside of Ellicott City, near Columbia. On the morning of February 7, Clark's son, James, noticed a bright light shining through his window and immediately alerted his parents, who

telephoned an alarm to the Ellicott City Fire Department. Since the fire started in the top floor, the Clarks and their neighbors were able to remove most of the furnishings before the flames consumed the rest of the house, but once again two familiar problems—the lack of an adequate water supply, combined with the head start the fire enjoyed by the time the Fire Company arrived—meant that the building itself could not be saved.

While the City Commissioners and the town's business leaders continued to debate the wisdom of purchasing a new fire engine, another blaze destroyed one of the businesses on the north side of Main Street, just east of Fel's Lane. Late on the morning of the last day of June 1922, a coal oil stove in the kitchen of Dr. James E. Shreeve—one of the town's leading dentists—caught fire. The flames spread at once to Dr. Shreeve's dental parlor, but the Fire Company arrived so promptly that the volunteers, under the direction of Police Chief Wosch, managed to keep the blaze from spreading to the home of Dr. William B. Gambrill next door.

Dr. Shreeve's losses, though serious, paled in comparison to the devastating destruction caused by a fire in January 1923 at Rock Hill College (3100 College Avenue). The boys' school, which had been built in 1830 under the original name of Rock Hill Academy (the name was changed to Rock Hill College in 1865 when it received its charter), had achieved international fame for its tradition of excellence. On the evening of January 16, the college chaplain, Reverend Michael A. Ryan, noticed bright flashes of light coming from the administration building. Reverend Ryan at once alerted several of the resident priests and called in an alarm. Some of the students tried to stop the spread of flames by dousing the fire with water carried in buckets from the college's pump, but the water soon gave out and the wind began to carry the fire throughout the building. By the time the Fire Company arrived, a huge crowd already had gathered on the scene, since the flames from the build-ing—which stood on a hill—could be seen for several miles. B. H. Shipley Jr., who was only eight years old at the time, remembered that night very well:

The night Rock Hill College burned in 1923, we were still living in Baltimore County, just across the river. We could hear the bell, and one of our neighbors said, "The college is on fire! We can see the flames." So my mother and I came over. My father had already gone to the fire, and after about an hour I said to my mother, "Let's go home," even though the thing was blazing and the fire was still growing. Nobody who knows me could imagine me doing this, but that's what I did.

Witnesses at the scene noticed that Ellicott City's fire engine obviously was inadequate to deal with a blaze of such magnitude. Once again, the equipment

Rock Hill College (3100 College Avenue). Bottom right: rear view of New Cut Road's two-unit log cabin, recently razed. Far left: St. Peter's Episcopal Church (St. Peter's Street).

arrived so late—the fire already had more than an hour's headway—that it already was out of control. Moreover, the water pressure at the scene was so low that the pumper could send only a small stream of water less than twenty feet into the air.

Once more, a disastrous fire prompted intensive discussions about the need to purchase modern firefighting equipment for Ellicott City and upgrade the city's water supply. This time, however, there was an added sense of urgency. Leading merchants and townspeople realized that a fire on a similarly windy night in downtown Ellicott City could have reduced the entire town to ashes. On the other hand, "many men are under the impression," claimed one observer, "that had an adequate supply of water been available last Tuesday night together with modern equipment, Rock Hill College could have been saved." Accordingly, a host of local companies—including the Patapsco National Bank, Easton's Sons, the *Ellicott City Times*, and John C. Maginnis—publicly pledged their support of a movement to obtain a motorized fire engine. Joining the drive were such prominent individuals as J. Booker Clark, Reverend Ryan of Rock Hill College, and James Clark, all of whom had suffered significantly from recent conflagrations. Since many of the most

damaging fires over the past few years had occurred outside the town limits, the leaders of the movement expressed their conviction that Howard County authorities ought to contribute to the purchase of new equipment as well.

It took another nightmarish incident, however, to persuade the town and county authorities to finally upgrade the Fire Company's equipment. On the night of Wednesday, November 21, 1923, a fire began in the chimney of the main building of the Patapsco Manor Sanitorium on College Avenue (Taylor Manor Hospital, 4110 College Avenue). Formerly the home of Thomas H. Gaither, Patapsco Manor—which had been used as a hospital since 1906—had already suffered one minor fire a year earlier which destroyed one of the sanitorium's smaller buildings. This time, however, the blaze threatened the entire hospital.

When the Ellicott City Fire Company received the alarm, the volunteers immediately hooked the horse-drawn engine to the back of the city's Model T Ford trash truck and headed for the fire. Careening down Main Street at top speed, the engine began to sway uncontrollably back and forth. Suddenly it caught a wheel in the groove of the trolley tracks in front of police headquarters, near the present site of Commercial and Farmers Bank;

breaking off from the truck, the fire engine overturned and plunged into a crowd of children who were standing on the pavement nearby.

Eight children were injured, and though most of them were treated at the scene and released, two received sufficiently severe injuries to require hospitalization. One child, a seven-year-old boy, was sent to St. Agnes Hospital in extremely serious condition.

Meanwhile, the sanitorium continued to burn. Although the Catonsville Fire Department responded to the alarm, the absence of any viable supply of water meant that they had no chance to control the blaze. The hospital's employees had removed most of its supplies from the main building before the fire consumed it, but once word of the fire spread throughout the area, a host of vandals gathered and began looting the pile of supplies, searching for drugs or liquor. Enraged, Dr. W. Rushmere White, the director of the sanitorium, grabbed a pistol and threatened to shoot anyone who tried to steal his supplies. In the ensuing confusion, however, hoodlums managed to steal more drugs before the Ellicott City and Baltimore County police finally restored order.

Now the authorities had no choice but to buy new firefighting apparatus. After the Patapsco Manor fiasco, the only fire extinguishers in the town were those owned by private residents. The loss of some of the finest residences of the county had shaken many property owners, and the constant need to call upon the firefighting companies of Baltimore County to assist in putting out even relatively minor fires was an embarrassment to both Ellicott City and Howard County officials.

On November 27, six days after the Patapsco Manor incident, two of the Ellicott City commissioners—Dr. Benjamin Mellor Jr. and Charles B. Wallenhorst—went to the Howard County Board of County Commissioners and asked for their help in financing the purchase of a modern fire engine for the city and county. A week later, Dr. Mellor and Milton H. Easton, the third City Commissioner, appeared before the County Commissioners with a representative of the American LaFrance Fire Engine Company and formally requested that the county help defray the cost—$10,500—of an American LaFrance engine.

The model that the American LaFrance representative recommended was a solid-tire, right-hand-drive, triple combination pumper-chemical-hose apparatus with a capacity of pumping seven hundred gallons of water per minute. The same seventy-five horse-power rotary motor used for driving the engine—a design which had proved far more reliable than the old Howe apparatus—would also be used for pumping water. According to the City Commissioners, the chemical attachment—a forty-gallon tank filled with water and bicarbonate of soda, to which was added sulphuric acid at the scene of the fire, thereby producing carbonic acid to smother the flames—was one of the key elements of the engine. Since nearly two-thirds of the fires at that time were extinguished with chemicals, this alleviated at least part of the difficulties of an inadequate water supply. Along with the engine and the hose, the truck would include ladders, hand extinguishers, fire axes, and pike poles.

One observer at the meeting was so impressed with the description of the new engine that he declared that "it is reasonably certain that the last half dozen fires within a radius of three or four miles of Ellicott City could have been extinguished promptly had this equipment been available here." To facilitate the work of the firefighters, farmers and residents of the county were urged to provide their own water reservoirs, such as dams, cisterns, or ice ponds on their property.

Dr. Mellor pointed out that he had done a thorough survey of the fire companies in Baltimore City and County, and many of them already used American LaFrance engines (in fact,

the proposed engine and hose was standardized with Baltimore County's equipment). Moreover, Baltimore County authorities had agreed to enter into reciprocal agreements for mutual assistance and the interchange of equipment during fire emergencies in either county. This meant that Howard County could expect help from up to four or five Baltimore County companies to fight major fires. Together with the extensive road improvement program upon which Howard County had recently embarked, the new engine promised to provide considerable relief to property owners in Ellicott City and the surrounding area.

To alleviate any remaining concerns, the County Commissioners traveled to Catonsville to meet with the chief of the Baltimore County Fire Department and inspect the Catonsville Department's American LaFrance equipment. Satisfied that the investment was a prudent one, the Commissioners subsequently agreed—with one dissenting vote from a disgruntled Commissioner who wanted Ellicott City to pay at least part of the engine's price—to purchase the American LaFrance engine. Payments would be made in three installments of $3,500 each, through a loan to the county by the Patapsco National Bank. Ellicott City Town Commissioners agreed to pay the interest on the two deferred payments. The haste with which the County Commissioners acted, considering the bureaucratic red tape which usually accompanied and delayed such decisions, testified to the urgency they felt in providing adequate fire protection for Howard County residents.

Before the new engine could arrive, however, another major fire struck one of Ellicott City's best-known residences. "Liburn," the three-story, twenty-room home of John C. Maginnis (3809 College Avenue) caught fire on the evening of December 16, 1923. Once again, the lack of competent fire-fighting equipment prevented volunteers from saving the seventy-year-old structure, though most of the furniture was rescued.

To fulfill its agreement with the county, the Ellicott City government agreed to provide a suitable structure to house the new fire engine, and to choose a competent engineer to operate it. The city subsequently purchased the E. A. Talbott Garage on Main Street, just west of the Talbott store (8316 Main Street), and remodeled the building so the engine could be sheltered on the first floor. The second floor was converted into an apartment where the Fire Company's chief engineer could

Miller Chevrolet Sales (8301 Hamilton Street), circa 1930.

live. That way, the authorities hoped, fire service would be immediately available day or night. As chief engineer, the city selected Mr. B. H. Shipley, who was employed as an auto mechanic by the nearby Green Cross Garage. (Green Cross subsequently was purchased by Charles E. Miller, who established Miller Chevrolet Sales on the site. Later, Miller Chevrolet Sales moved to the western edge of town.)

A native of Ellicott City, whose parents had moved here several decades earlier, B. H. Shipley already had been active in the affairs of the Volunteer Fire Company. When the Company still operated its horse-drawn equipment, Mr. Shipley had been responsible—if he was available when an alarm came in—for hooking the apparatus onto a gasoline-powered truck and driving it to the site of the fire. Before 1924, Mr. Shipley had resided across the Patapsco River, in the section of Ellicott City that was in Baltimore County. When the new engine arrived in June 1924, he moved into the apartment with his wife, Mary ("May"), and their young son, B. H. Shipley Jr.

The original firehouse would later be used by Ellicott City for municipal purposes, until it was sold to the Howard County Board of County Commissioners in 1935. From the summer of 1935 until the spring of 1962, the county used the building to house the offices of the Howard County Welfare Board; then it became the home of the Sanitation Division of the Howard County Health Department. In 1969, the site became a branch of the Howard County Public Library. Finally, the building was restored to its original design in 1989–90, and became the Firehouse Museum, housing historical artifacts, photographs, documents, and clothing relating to the colorful past of firefighting.

As part of their modernization program in 1924, the Ellicott City Fire Department also decided to change the name of the organization to The Volunteer Firemen of Howard County. This signified its intention to serve the entire county, and transformed the company into a more efficient organization. At a meeting on June 10, new officers were selected: Edward A. Rodey (the proprietor of Amusea Theater—the town's silent movie theater) as presi-

Underwriters test, drafting water from the Old Mill Race, first motorized pumper, June 1924.

Baltimore County Fire Department "Packard" chief's car with mounted deck gun on rear. Underwriters June test of Engine No. 1.

A. McNabb its lieutenants.

The Company hoped to enlist the service of eighteen to twenty men as volunteer firefighters, but since so many residents of Ellicott City worked in Baltimore City during the day, the daytime volunteer force obviously would have to consist of young men who worked in Howard County. Since the Fire Department would have the responsibility of responding to calls throughout the county, the Company decided not to require its members to live within the Ellicott City limits.

Shortly thereafter, the Fire Department also launched a training

dent, G. Ray Helm as vice president, Leonard A. McNabb as secretary, and Richard Talbott as treasurer. The Volunteer Fire Company No. 1 chose Dr. Benjamin Mellor Jr. as its new chief. (Chief Mellor owned one of the most distinctive automobiles in Ellicott City—an Essex "cheesebox," which he would drive to the scene of fires). The Company also selected B. H. Shipley as chief engineer, assisted by Frank K. Collette and Preston P. Miller. The Company named H. O. Makinson its captain, and Charles E. Delosier, G. Ray Helm, Edward S. McNabb, and Leonard

Edward A. Rodey proprietor (8048 Main Street), former Ellicott City postmaster, president of the Volunteer Fire Company of Howard County. Mr. Rodey was active in civic affairs, especially the Federal Government's W.P.A. projects in the Ellicott City area.

program, deliberately setting fires under controlled conditions, to provide its volunteers with additional experience.

As part of the reorganization process, the Fire Department also revised its alarm procedures. At the end of June 1924, it informed the public that anyone who wished to turn in a fire alarm should call the central telephone operator at 236, who would then transfer the call to Mr. Shipley's apartment. "He had a telephone extension off of the line," recalled B. H. Shipley Jr., "so that when the phone rang, and if it was a fire call, he could say to my mother, 'May, I got it.' " Then, while Mr. Shipley got the fire engine ready for action, his wife would call Charles E. Buetefisch, who owned a tailor shop and residence near the old firehouse where the bell was still located. Mr. Buetefisch would then go over and ring the bell, alerting the firemen.

The 236 phone number remained in use for only one year. It was a party line, and was busy on several occasions when emergencies occurred. In 1925, therefore, the number was changed to a private line—232. Emergency calls went directly to the firehouse. The operator did not take the emergency information; rather, she merely answered the call and plugged the caller directly into the firehouse line. Someone was always available at the station to answer emergency calls. The Ellicott City Volunteer Firemen's Association has continued to use the 232 combination of numbers in its business telephone number (410-465-0232) through the present day.

Since the fire equipment had to cover both the town and the county, the Fire Department needed different signals to inform the volunteers where the fire was located. If the fire were in the town itself, the bell sounded a continuous ringing, as it always had. If the fire were in the county, the bell tolled five taps repeated five times, with an interval of ten seconds between every five taps. For a fire drill, the alarm sounded three taps five times. Because dozens of people called to seek the location of a blaze, telephone operators also announced that they would no longer provide details of fires to curiosity-seekers. Reportedly so many calls had flooded the switchboards that normal telephone service frequently was impaired.

Despite the revised regulations, a sizable crowd gathered to watch the newly reorganized Fire Department respond to its first call June 23. Shortly after two o'clock in the afternoon the fire alarm sounded, and within minutes Mr. Shipley and a crew of volunteers were heading west on Frederick Pike in the American LaFrance engine. Less than ten minutes later, they had extinguished the flames leaping out of a farm truck, laden with produce, that had caught fire in front of the Enterprise Garage—formerly the H. Oldfield Pump Works (8602 Frederick Road). Using only their chemical reserve, the firefighters put out the blaze easily, saving the farmer's produce and earning con-

Hamilton Oldfield Pump Works (8602 Frederick Road). Later occupants were Green Cross Garage, Enterprise Motor Car Company, and West End Service, Inc.

siderable applause from the onlookers.

The Fire Company still needed additional equipment, especially new turnout gear—protective coat, protective pants and boots—to help protect the firefighters from the cold while spraying water on a fire. To raise funds, the Company decided to sponsor a carnival, while simultaneously making a direct appeal to local residents and businessmen. Accordingly, President Edward A. Rodey of the Volunteer Fire Company of Howard County asked the

Ellicott City Times to print a message in its July 3, 1924, issue, reminding taxpayers that their cooperation was essential to the establishment of an effective firefighting force. "There is positively one thing we must have," noted Rodey. "YOUR COOPERATION. We have at this time approximately twenty-five men offering their services gratis, to fight fires at any time and place within the confines of Howard County, and from my personal observation of their work on past occasions, I know they will carry out this pledge and ask no favors." But, he continued, "if we are going to expect of them this hazard in our behalf [we need] TO SEE THAT THEY ARE PROPERLY EQUIPPED TO MEET ALL EMERGENCIES."

The first Firemen's Carnival since its reorganization, which took place September 3-6, 1924, at Maryland Avenue (Depot Yard) proved a huge success. Even though the weather turned unseasonably chilly, the crowd surpassed the expectations of the planners, and the Company netted more than $2,500 in receipts. Visitors to the carnival were presented with souvenir programs emblazoned with the motto of the Company—"SERVICE—ANYWHERE—ANYTIME"—and a photograph of the active members of Engine and Hose Company No. 1 standing in front of the American LaFrance engine. By that time, the Company had divided the volunteers into a "chemical department," consisting of Thomas Lilly, Sydney J. Hyatt, L. Burgess Wamsley, and T. Hunt Mayfield Jr., all of whom had the responsibility of working the chemical tanks, and teams of "hosemen," including William S. Hodges, John H. Lyons, Albert Greenwood, Carl Thompson, Adam Noll, J. Raymond Meldron, Addison Hodges, Nathan Hunt, Lester Mullineaux, John Laumann, Elmer C. Cavey, and Harrison Yates.

The Company explained to carnival-goers that its goal was to raise sufficient funds to obtain a chemical engine for each district in Howard County. Toward that end, President Rodey of the Volunteer Fire Company of Howard County went again to the County Commissioners to enlist their support for this effort. "While the new American LaFrance engine was a vast improvement over the previous Howe engine," President Rodey noted, "drivers still had difficulty navigating the heavy engine over Howard County roads, many of which were still in poor condition." The Commissioners responded by approving the formation of a committee of three County Commissioners, three Ellicott City

Commissioners, and three representatives of the Volunteer Firemen to devise a plan to accomplish their goal. The following month, Edward A. Rodey, Dr. Benjamin Mellor Jr., and H. O. Makinson returned to the Commissioners and informed them that J. Booker Clark had graciously presented the Company with an International chassis that had been used as a coal truck. The Company now wished to use the balance of proceeds from the carnival to obtain and outfit the chassis with two forty-gallon soda and acid tanks, thereby giving the county two engines with chemical firefighting capabilities.

Since the arrangement cost the county virtually nothing except the purchase of two forty-gallon copper soda and acid chemical tanks, the Commissioners readily gave their blessings. Working with two other volunteer firemen (Preston P. Miller and Albert Parks), and a local blacksmith (Howard B. Courts), Chief Engineer B. H. Shipley outfitted the chassis with the tanks and added a portable pump which could be carried down to a local stream or branch to supplement the water supply at the scene of a fire. The new engine (known to the firemen as "Little Kate" and "Puddle Jumper") would subsequently become the Volunteer Fire Company's most frequently used apparatus, since the county's continuing problems with inadequate water supplies often rendered the American LaFrance pumper ineffective. It was first used that summer for a brush fire on the evening of July 4, which had started when someone threw a lighted sparkler into the brush on the hillside at the intersection of Main Street and Church Road during the Independence Day celebration.

Now that their firefighting equipment was motorized, the Fire Company found itself considerably busier than it had ever been, responding to emergencies over a far wider range of territory. During their first year of service, the Volunteer Firemen of Howard County responded to thirty-five alarms: twelve were fires in fields, barns, or woods; sixteen more were house fires, including twelve that began in chimneys; and three involved vehicle fires. Three of the chimney fires occurred in the space of a several weeks in December, leading the Fire Department to urge residents to have their chimneys cleaned before the cold weather arrived in earnest. During another hectic week in April, the Company responded to five separate alarms: a chimney fire in a house on Fel's Lane, a roof/chimney blaze in a house at Orange Grove, a field fire on the property of James B. Clark, a wood fire near Highland, and a blaze in

one of the outbuildings at St. Paul's Parochial School.

As a result of the increased frequency of alarms, the Fire Department decided in mid-April 1925 that it would not send the fire engine to fight field and brush fires unless the flames threatened nearby buildings. If any buildings were endangered, however, the Department urged residents to call in alarms promptly if they believed the Fire Company could render service.

The enhanced range of the American LaFrance fire engine also highlighted another problem: the failure of motorists to grant the right-of-way to the fire truck when it was responding to an alarm. The penalty for failing to move aside involved suspension of a driver's license for thirty to sixty days. More severe was the consequence suffered by one obstinate driver who refused to yield to the fire truck on a warm day in June. When the motorist stubbornly failed to heed the warning of the fire gong on the engine—which was heading to a fire at a farm house in Alpha—he caused a three-car accident when the vehicles reached the intersection of Frederick Road and Manor Lane.

In responding to calls throughout Howard County, the volunteer firemen also subjected themselves to considerable physical hardships. During a blinding snowstorm on a bitterly cold afternoon at the end of January 1925, the Fire Company responded to an alarm from the old Glenwood Institute, which had been converted to a private home and boardinghouse known as "The Maples," owned by Mrs. Elizabeth Dorsey. Eleven firemen responded to the call, including Dr. Benjamin Mellor Jr., who recently had been elected chief by the members of the Company, B. H. Shipley, T. Hunt Mayfield, Preston P. Miller, Charles E. Delosier, and Leonard A. McNabb. Most of the men rode the fifteen miles to Glenwood through the snow and sleet on the open truck, which traveled at an average speed of twenty-five to thirty miles an hour. By the time they arrived, their faces, hands, and feet were suffering from the extreme cold. Since the fire already had completely destroyed the house before the firemen arrived, they had to turn around and make the return trip at once through the cold and snow. Three of the firemen suffered frozen ears from the painful journey, and several others reported severely swollen hands and feet. None of them complained, however, and when one of the stricken men was asked how he felt, he answered, "I am ready for the next call." Still, the firefighters had been angered by the treatment afforded them by the people

of Glenwood. When one resident at the scene of the fire put his hands over the fire engine's radiator that was still warm from the long drive from Ellicott City, a firefighter threatened to smack his hand with a hammer if he didn't get it off of the radiator right away. Upon the return of the firefighters, the *Ellicott City Times* expressed its outrage that the people of Glenwood had not even offered the men hot cups of coffee to warm them before their return trip. "These young men give their time and effort to the people of Howard County GRATIS," the newspaper reminded county residents, "and the least that can be expected in return is a little HUMAN TREATMENT. A pat on the back is fine for encouragement, but it does not put a hot cup of coffee in the stomachs of a bunch of half frozen men. These men are entitled to the best that can be given when they turn out to protect any man's home."

The most devastating fire of the Volunteer Firemen's first year, however, was the conflagration that struck the town of Mount Airy June 4, 1925. For decades, the residents of Mt. Airy had known that their town lacked an adequate water supply; in fact, a fire in 1903 had nearly destroyed the entire town. But the voters had rejected a bond issue for fire protection in 1914, and even though they had approved a smaller bond issue in 1917 following another major fire, the funds had been exhausted before a water system could be installed. Another bond issue specifically designed to provide an adequate water supply was subsequently passed, but a persistent argument over access to springs at the source of the water supply prevented the installation of a large 75,000-gallon water tank.

On the evening of June 4, the scarcity of water again hampered the efforts of the Howard County firefighters, who were joined by firemen from Frederick, Rockville, and Kensington. The fire engines were forced to pump water from locomotive tender tanks which hauled water to the scene of the fire, thereby preventing any further spread of the blaze. Despite their best efforts, however, most of the town north of the railroad tracks—about half of the business district of Mt. Airy—was completely destroyed; estimates of the damage ranged as high as $200,000. Gone were the First National Bank Building, the Odd Fellows Building, a grain mill, a merchandise store, two grocery stores, an electrician's shop, a hardware and furniture store, and several additional frame buildings.

The lack of water also frustrated the firefighters' attempts to extinguish a fire at the home of William Fulton on Fairview Farm, in Hilton (Old Columbia Pike and Montgomery Road), in late February. Once again, the fire apparently began in a defective chimney flue in the attic and had gained considerable headway by the time the firefighters arrived. "Due to the spread of the flames and the lack of water," lamented one fireman, "we were forced to stand by and see the fine residence destroyed by the flames."

Summer brought a different set of seasonal problems for the firefighters. During this period, fireworks were still legal in Maryland, and most residents of Ellicott City celebrated the Fourth of July with their own private fireworks displays. Not surprisingly, several fires resulted from errant sparks during the Independence Day festivities in the summer of 1925, including two which could have resulted in significant damage had not the fire company responded with promptness. In one case, the dry underbrush between Main Street and the courthouse caught fire, threatening the adjacent buildings with destruction before the firefighters extinguished the flames.

Around ten o'clock that evening, a second fire occurred on the roof of a house on Fel's Lane. Although the firemen brought this blaze, too, under control, there were still smoldering sparks which could have developed into full-fledged fires during the night. Fortunately, a band of showers arrived just before midnight, soaking the town and eliminating any further danger. The evening also was marred by a series of fireworks-related accidents, including a serious facial injury to one of the town's residents. As a result of these incidents, local authorities subsequently decided to stage a community fireworks display, in hopes that individuals might forego their own, more dangerous celebrations.

In August 1925, the Volunteer Fire Company of Howard County held its second annual carnival—this time on the campus of the recently-completed Ellicott City High School (at 3700 College Avenue), so they could have more room for all the displays and entertainments that had been restricted for lack of space the previous summer. Starting with a parade led by the Evening Sun Newsboys' Band, the event was, according to reports, "the biggest carnival ever held in these parts." The Company proudly reported that its ranks of active members had grown to twenty-eight men, not count-ing the eleven officers. It also reminded residents that they should now tele-phone fire alarms to "Ellicott City 232": State your Name, Location of Fire and Survey Number, giving any Information Possible as to Nature of Fire, Condition

Angelo Cottage on the side of "Tarpein Rock" (3749 Church Road)— built in the 1830s. For eight years, in the 1840s, the cottage was the pastoral residence for the priests from St. Paul's Church.

of Roads, also Available Water Supply." The purpose of the carnival was to raise funds to supplement the appropriations for equipment made by the County Commissioners and the Commissioners of Ellicott City. Occasionally, grateful property owners endeavored to pay the firefighters for their services, but no such payments were accepted.

Clearly the activities of the Fire Company represented one of the major sources of entertainment in Ellicott City in those days. For every fire alarm that sounded, an average of fifteen to twenty people called the firehouse to find out where the fire was. Finally, the Fire Department had to put a notice in the *Times* asking residents not to tie up the telephone lines with such calls, since they were "proving to be a serious handicap in the dispatch of the engines."

In their second year since reorganiz-ing as the Volunteer Firemen of Howard County, the Fire Company responded to even more alarms than they had in 1924–25. In fact, they answered more than thirty-five alarms between January 1 and the end of April, including a record seven calls during one week in mid-April. Nor did the pace of alarms abate in the ensuing months. By May, the volunteers had developed an efficient routine that allowed them to leave the engine house with "Big Kate," as they fondly dubbed the American LaFrance engine, within three minutes of receiving an alarm. The International chemical engine, known as "Little Kate," also was kept busy. In the spring of 1926, for instance, the Company called it into service thirty times within a two-month period.

Despite the hectic pace of firefighting activity, Ellicott City remained a relatively stable community in the 1920s. There was little construction along Main Street. The town had a public water supply, but it was not an adequate and reliable water supply for fire protection. Ellicott City authorities also provided police protection, along with street maintenance and trash pick-up within the town limits. Trash pickup was performed by a one-man crew operating a Model T Ford truck with a dump body. The trash collector (in the 1920s, a gentleman named William Teal) would pick up the trash and deposit it along the roadside between a stream bank and New Cut Road, approximately six hundred feet south-west of the intersection of St. Paul Street and New Cut Road. The town Commissioners also permitted residents to dump metal—such as automobile fenders and bodies—along the bank of a stream running along New Cut Road, about seventy-five feet southwest of 3776 St. Paul Street. (Both former dumping areas are now posted "Private Parking.")

In the early years of the decade, the Ellicott City Elementary and High School was located on what was then known as School Street and Strawberry Lane (3673 Park Avenue). Because of space constraints, the first and second grade classes formerly had been held in the Old Friends' Meeting House (3771 Old Columbia Pike) about one-fourth mile away. During the 1920–21 school year, however, two temporary buildings were constructed at the high school so the first two primary grades could be housed at the same location. At the time, this was the only high school in the county, with about twenty students in each graduating class. Students who lived in Elkridge or Woodstock had to ride the train to get to school.

In 1925, a new Ellicott City Elementary and High School was constructed at 3700 College Avenue. Water for the school was supplied from Rock Hill Reservoir at Forty Acres (3940 New Cut Road) formerly used by Rock Hill College. The system had not been used since the college was destroyed by fire on January 16, 1923. Finding the supply inadequate and unreliable, it became necessary to drill a well to the rear of the school building. Solid rock had to be penetrated, and after six or seven weeks, a well was drilled to the depth of 287 feet and about February 25, 1928, a supply of good, pure water had been secured flowing up to twenty-four gallons per minute.

High school students remained at the College Avenue location until a new high school was built in 1939 on 4445 Montgomery Road (Ellicott Mills Middle School). Elementary pupils remained at the College Avenue location until 1976, when they moved to their present location at Worthington Elementary School at 4570 Round Hill Road.

During the 1920s, schools in Ellicott City were racially segregated, as were schools in most of Maryland. The Ellicott City black elementary school was a one-room frame building located along the Hudson Branch, near the intersection of Frederick Road and Rogers Avenue. At that time, the

school had no drinking water. Until a well and pump were installed in 1950, students had to carry water to school from their homes. For heat, the school had to rely on pot-bellied stoves, which burned coal and wood. With no indoor plumbing, the students and the two teachers—one for the primary grades, and the other for grades four through seven—had to use the two outhouses behind the school. In 1953, the town's black students relocated to a new building at 3676 Fel's Lane. Following the desegregation of Howard County schools in the early 1960s, the Howard County Police Department moved their headquarters from the second firehouse location (at 8316 Main Street) into the Fel's Lane school building on September 28, 1964. After the police department relocated its headquarters to its present location in the Warfield Building at 3410 Court House Drive, the county's Parks and Recreation Department established the Roger Carter Neighborhood Center on the site of the former school building.

There were also private schools in Ellicott City during the 1920s. Perhaps the most prominent was St. Paul's Parochial School at 3475 St. Paul Street. Before the school opened, the property had been the site of the first Patapsco National Bank Building. The

St. Paul's Roman Catholic Church (3755 St. Paul Street)—original church completed and blessed in 1838. Bell weighing 555 pounds was placed in tower in 1844. Steeple built in 1896.

and Sunday School room. In 1966, students in both St. Paul's schools were transferred to the St. Paul the Apostle School, at 3175 Paulskirk Drive. Three decades later, the school had become an inner parish school known as Resurrection/St. Paul's School.

The list of Ellicott City's churches during the 1920s included St. Paul's Roman Catholic Church at the present address of 3755 St. Paul's Street, St. Peter's Episcopal Church on St. Peter Street (St. Paul's Place), the First Lutheran Church (3761 Church Road), Emory M. E. Church (3799 Church Road), First Presbyterian Church (8328 Court Avenue), St. Luke's A. M. E. Church

Bank subsequently sold the lot to a Mr. Isaac. It was then purchased by Mr. Daniel D. Hewett. St. Paul's gained possession of the property May 1, 1921. Following renovations to the building, the school opened in September 1922 for students in grades one through six.

St. Paul's also operated a parochial school for black students on St. Peter's Street (now St. Paul Place). The school opened in the mid-1920s in a building that formerly had been used as a hall

First Presbyterian Church, "Capitoline Hill" (8320 Court Avenue)—completed in 1844, front wall collapsed in April 1894. Rebuilt with dedication December 23, 1894, circa 1890.

Emory Methodist Episcopal Church (3799 Church Road)—back is facing Main Street. Dedicated January 23, 1888, circa 1890.

(8411 Frederick Road), the First Baptist Church of Ellicott City (8465 Frederick Road), and the Mt. Zion A. M. E. Methodist Church (8565 Frederick Road). St. Peter's was subsequently destroyed by fire, and in later decades the First Lutheran and First Presbyterian churches both relocated. On February 21, 1984, the walls of the First Baptist Church, which had been built in 1914 and had long since been abandoned, finally collapsed, leading authorities to order the building razed to avoid a further safety hazard.

Since Howard County was still a farming community, residents of Ellicott City did not find it surprising to look out and see herds of cattle being driven to market down Main Street or Columbia Avenue (Old Columbia Pike), then to Maryland Avenue and Mulligan Hill (Mullicans Hill Lane), where there was a loading pen to move

them onto the freight rail cars. Most of the cattle, however, were driven all the way into Baltimore by way of Frederick Avenue. "I also remember wagon loads of wheat parked on Main Street," noted B. H. Shipley Jr., "stretching almost up to Columbia Avenue (Old Columbia Pike), waiting to be unloaded, because they had to be dumped one bag at a time."

Main Street itself—whose cobble-stones disappeared in 1922 when it was repaved in concrete—was lined with

First Baptist Church (8465 Frederick Road)— built in 1914, crumbled to the ground Tuesday, February 21, 1984, with debris spilling into the street blocking traffic.

businesses, all of which were owned by white residents, with the exception of one black barber. In all, the town possessed eight grocery stores, eight churches, and six garages (some for the sale of new cars, and others for repairs and storage) along with two drugstores, two banks, and four coal supply houses, most of whom had to unload their coal on the B & O Railroad siding along Maryland Avenue and Mulligan Hill (Mullicans Hill Lane). Under the B & O railroad tracks, there was also a three-foot-wide granite pier in the center of Main Street, holding the railroad's steel girders in place. The pier, which was owned by the railroad, presented a substantial traffic problem, since westbound trucks couldn't maneuver through the curve from Baltimore County. Instead, they had to go in the eastbound lane in front of oncoming traffic. Although a Howard County grand jury recommended the removal of the pier in March 1920, it was not removed until July 1931.

Many of the Ellicott City business owners lived on upper floors above their shops or offices. At the bottom of Main Street, on the southern side at the intersection with Maryland Avenue, the business district began with a women's apparel store known as the "Mary Helen Shop," followed by a barbershop, both of which were torn down decades later

when local authorities decided to widen the Maryland Avenue entrance to Main Street to alleviate persistent traffic congestion. At the present site of 8049 Main Street stood a confectionery owned by Walter S. Fissell. Like most of the town's confectioneries, Fissell's sold sandwiches and light lunch fare along with candy and sodas. The remaining structures on that block were occupied by J. H. Kramer's Grocery Store and the Easton Sons' Funeral Parlor.

Edward T. Clark operated a farm supply store which had, in years past, offered such arcane services as placing leg irons on the prisoners in the county jail. Adjacent to Clark's was the Coroneos Brothers' Confectionery, followed by the Kraft Brothers' Meat Market, Frank Fisher's Barbershop, another confectionery—this one owned by the Valmas Brothers—and Rosenstock's Department Store. Then came Thomas Brian's Grocery Store, and a barbershop owned by Phillip A. Laumann, who was one of the original members of Fire Company No. 1, and a diehard Republican. Sometimes an unwary customer engaged Laumann in a political discussion, and if the debate grew too heated, Laumann would simply refuse to finish shaving his lathered client. Next came Caplan's Department Store—still a landmark on Main Street in the

1990s—and Kirkwood's Footwear (where one could purchase ready-made boots and shoes), followed by another grocery owned by W. H. Fissell.

Next to Fissell's, at the present 8139 Main Street, stood the Washington Trust Company of Maryland, one of the town's two full-service banks. The rest of the block consisted of Wise & Hope's housewares and appliance store, the Ellicott City Community Market, a clothing store, Loughran's bakery, Johnson's pharmacy (which had been damaged during the 1917 fire), the Chesapeake and Potomac Telephone Company Exchange and Office, the American Stores grocery, the U.S. Post Office (in its remodeled offices two doors down from its previous site, which had also been destroyed by fire in 1917), the Atlantic & Pacific Tea Company—the only retail grocery chain store in town—and Taylor's Furniture and Jewelry Store. Above the A & P, Dr. Louis L. Brown, one of the town's numerous dentists, had an office.

There were three pathways from Main Street to the Tiber Branch in the 8100 block of Main Street. One pathway ran between Laumann's Barbershop and Caplan's Department Store; another between the market and Wise & Hope's, and a third between Johnson's Pharmacy and the C & P Telephone Company. (The first pathway has since been blocked, although there are outside stairs to the second floor, and the second was closed off prior to a major fire in 1984.)

At the intersection of Main Street and Columbia Avenue (Old Columbia Pike) stood the Central Grocery, owned

by James Steward. In 1925, the Standard Oil Company purchased the lot, tore down the grocery, and built a filling station. At the time, the *Ellicott City Times* reported that the demolition of the old three-story building that housed the grocery store, and its replacement by the filling station, was "one of the greatest real estate improvements, from a public viewpoint, which has taken place in Ellicott City recently." (Forty years later, the filling station would be torn down to permit officials to widen the intersection of Main Street and Columbia Pike.)

James Steward's Central Grocery three-story building— Main Street and Columbia Avenue. Razed in 1925.

Aesthetic improvements covered the unsightly wall that remained after the filling station was razed and removed in 1964.

Adjacent to Steward's was the lunchroom run by William F. Lilly & Son. Above the restaurant, Lilly—who was active in the affairs of the Firemen's Association—ran a pocket billiard parlor. At the present address of 8225 Main Street, Der Wong, one of the town's few Chinese residents, operated a laundry service. Moving further up the street, shoppers arrived at William E. Mayfield's Saddlery and Harness Store, August Stigler's Bakery and the tailor shop of Charles E. Buetefisch (the gentleman who was responsible for ringing the fire bell upon a signal from the Shipleys until 1927). On election day, Buetefisch's shop also

served as the local polling place, as town officials draped a white curtain over a board to serve as a voting booth.

Next to Buetefisch's shop stood Stigler's Plumbing Services and Samuel J. Yates' Grocery Store. At 8267 Main Street, the street-level address was occupied by a service station. The town's Ford sales and service shop, Ellicott City Motors, occupied 8289 Main Street, adjacent to the office of Dr. M. Gist Sykes, one of Ellicott City's leading dentists and one of the original officers of Volunteer Fire Company No. 1. During this period, new automobiles would arrive in town

Mayfield Saddlery and Harness Store (8227 Main Street). On left William F. Mayfield and on right Charles "Uncle Charlie" McCummesky who at the time of his death—January 23, 1934—was the oldest living volunteer fireman in the State of Maryland. He would have been 102 in late February 1934. In front is Walter C. Edmonston.

by train, and would be unloaded by the B & O Railroad siding along Maryland Avenue. The new Fords would be taken up the hill to the Ellicott City Motors and the new Chevrolets would be taken up the hill to Green Cross Garage.

Continuing up the street, one came to the home of A. Victor Weaver, next to the open stream of the Hudson Branch of the Patapsco. Finally, at 8385 Main Street, Olivia Frost ran a dry goods store, and P. N. Ditch operated a confectionery. Next to the confectionery stood Andrew Martin's blacksmith shop; on the second floor of this shop was a silent movie hall for the town's black residents. The site of Martin's blacksmith shop was later purchased by Charles E. Miller, who demolished the house and shop and constructed a filling station. Mr. Miller

subsequently sold the filling station to Roger C. Wall. In later years, it was purchased by the Fire Department for use as an annex building.

The north side of Main Street provided fewer shops and more professional offices. Down by the Patapsco River, on Frederick Road, stood the Lord Baltimore Filling Station. McDonald's General Merchandise Store stood on Oella Avenue. On the site of the present "Parking Lot A," the New Coal and Supply Company sold coal. On Main Street itself, the business district began with the Bridge Market, a general merchandise store, followed by an ice plant and Howard Council No. 46, the meeting hall where one of the local fraternal orders (the Junior Orders) held its meetings. Amusea Theater, Ellicott City's silent movie theater—practically the only entertainment in town apart from the Fire Department's annual car-

enforcement officer since his appointment as constable in 1904—continued in his post as chief of police. Chief Wosch (an imposing-looking man who was then in his fifties) had his own unique and somewhat informal, but extremely effective method of handling miscreants. "He was not only the police," recalls B. H. Shipley Jr., "he was everything here. Nowadays you'd call him a city administrator. His office was diagonally across from where Commercial and Farmer's Bank is now. He had an old Maxwell automobile. It made a terrible noise and people could hear him coming. Instead of starting up his car, he'd stop a trolley and get on. And then when the trolley pulled into the terminus at Main Street and Fel's Lane, he'd get off and catch the wrongdoers. Then he'd say to them, 'You go up to jail. I'll call Mr. Charles Cumberland [he was the warden] and I'll tell him you're coming,' and up there he would go."

"The fines used to be $6.45 or $11.45. Sometimes they'd say to the

nivals and an occasional Chataqua stage show held at the courthouse—occupied the fifth floor of the town hall (8044–8046 Main Street), next to Charles Yates' Grocery Store and the newsstand of Edward A. Rodey, the owner of the theater and the first president of the Volunteer Firemen of Howard County. Rounding out the block were the extensive showrooms of the Patapsco Furniture Store, the Patapsco Pharmacy, and the Patapsco National Bank, Ellicott City's other full-service financial institution.

At the next block stood the police headquarters and the judicial offices of Justice Frank C. Higinbothom, the town's trial magistrate. During the 1920s, Julius Wosch—who had served as Ellicott City's only full-time law magistrate, 'I don't have the money.' He'd say, 'Pay me Friday.' " At that time, the jail—known as Willow Grove, or "Stoney Lonesome"—was located at the site of the current sheriff's office. "We used to play ball as kids in the field there," recalls Mr. Shipley with a chuckle. "That's all fill dirt there, and the well and pump house for the Patapsco Institute was back there. That was later all covered over when they cut in Courthouse Drive."

"There was a tennis court back there, too. During prohibition, federal prisoners were assigned here. The warden, Mr. Charles Cumberland, would let them out, and they'd go down the street and buy steaks and things, because they didn't like the food he was providing. He'd also let them out to play ball with us, and they bought us balls and gloves. And whenever we had a carnival, he'd let them go to the car-

Howard County Jail with a frame addition for use as the warden's residence and office.

nival, and then they'd go back to jail."

Lawbreakers who had committed more appalling crimes would receive a stiffer penalty, but there had been no executions in Ellicott City since the last public hanging in 1916, and there would be no more in the future. From that time on, the county jail was used only to imprison criminals on less severe charges, or to confine accused individuals who were awaiting trial.

Further up the block from police headquarters were the shoe repair shops of A. M. Kropp and Joseph Novicki. Next came the insurance offices of Charles A. Herrmann and George W. Carr—both of whom had been longtime members of Ellicott City's Fire Department—Centre Lodge No. 40 (the meeting place of the local chapter of the International Order of Odd Fellows), and the offices of the *Ellicott City Times*, owned by the Maryland Printing and Publishing Company. Rounding out the block were the insurance and real estate offices of Dorsey M. Williams, Frank Scott's Barber Shop (the only Main Street establishment owned by a black man), F. C. Higinbothom's Funeral Parlor, which was established in 1929, and another barber shop, owned by Charles Meade.

At the present site of 8202 Main Street stood the Howard House, frequently occupied by Baltimore City dwellers who wanted to journey all the way out to rural Howard County for their summer vacation. In fact, the Howard House—with its famous iron grille work on the second floor facade—took up most of its block. Although Christian Eckert still owned the Howard House, by the mid-1920s he had turned over much of the daily operation of the hotel to John and Catherine Reichenbecker.

Besides serving as a favorite resting place and restaurant for local residents and visitors, frequently featuring German-American dishes on the menu, the peculiar configuration of the Howard House also allowed it to serve as a passageway for local residents who wished to go from Main Street to the county courthouse, which stood on a hill behind the hotel. Since the hotel was built on a steep, rocky hillside, one could enter the hotel at the Main Street entrance, walk up several flights of stairs, and exit on the level of the rear street. During the late nineteenth century, Eckert had also owned the property across from the hotel, where he oper-

ated a soft drink plant. Throughout the county, Eckert had earned a reputation for making the best ice cream in the region, reportedly turning out more than two thousand gallons some summers for the enjoyment of his customers and local residents.

The Starr Funeral Home was in the next block, west of Church Road. In the present 8300 block of Main Street, visitors would find Edward Alexander Talbott's Lumber and Coal Yard, the fire engine house, the office of Dr. Frank O. Miller, Edward Pickett's Grocery Store, Dr. William B. Gambrill's office, the dental offices of Dr. James F. Shreeve, and a vacant lot owned by the Makinson family. Finally, the terminus of the United Railway and Electric Company, the town's trolley line, occupied the site of the present Fire Department parking lot.

On the north side of Frederick Road, prospective automobile buyers found the Kerger Motor Company, where they could inspect the newest Dodge automobiles or obtain service on a recent purchase; the Burgess Garage (formerly the Burgess Carriage and Wagon Works), where the latest models of Buicks were on display; and the Enterprise Motor Car Company, which repaired and provided storage space for cars. Between Burgess and Enterprise was sandwiched

Burgess Carriage and Wagon Works (8444 Frederick Road). Mrs. Samuel Burgess in April 1925 gave permission to the Ellicott City Fire Department to repair the abandoned race off the Hudson Branch and extend a standpipe to Frederick Road to be used as a water supply in case of fire.

Robert G. Yates' florist shop.

One of the most important buildings in Ellicott City, as far as the Volunteer Fire Company was concerned, was the Green Cross Garage, where Chief Engineer Shipley was employed. From January 1916 to December 1917, the Green Cross Garage—then under the management of Edward S. Warfield— operated a Chevrolet dealership in the closed H. Oldfield's Pump Works (8602 Frederick Road). In 1917 the company purchased the Stephen Hillsinger & Son Livery Stable that was constructed over the Tiber Branch in the 1870s. One side of the building was on Hamilton Street (8301 Hamilton Street) and the other side was on Columbia Avenue (3726 Old Columbia Road). From 1918 to 1929, the garage provided sales and service for automobiles. Cars that needed repairs were taken to the second floor of the garage by way of a ramp leading from the Columbia Avenue side of the building. If an automobile could not be driven up the ramp, a rope attached to a winch mounted near the front of the shop was used to raise the car to the second floor. On the west side of the building, an addition (which did not extend over the Tiber Branch) housed the garage's office and parts department. From 1918

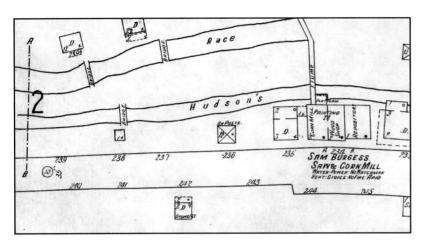

Burgess Carriage and Wagon Works race.

to 1929, the garage also operated a gasoline pump, dispensing "Wizard" brand gas. The pump was located on the corner of Main and Hamilton Streets, near Samuel J. Yates' Grocery Store.

After Edward Warfield was called into the military service during World War I, Melville Scott was named manager of the Green Cross Garage. After

1929, Mr. Scott went into the insurance business, opening an insurance office under the name of Melville Scott & Son in the Times Building at 8156 Main Street. From 1929 to 1936, Miller Chevrolet Sales occupied the garage building before relocating to 8307 Main Street. The garage building subsequently was used as a machine shop by the Doughnut Corporation of America. Later it became a warehouse for Taylor's Furniture Store. Finally, an arson fire destroyed the building and its contents on the night of March 5, 1992.

During the 1920s, Ellicott City's official limits extended west to Robert G. Yates' florist shop (now 8452 Frederick Road), south on Columbia Avenue to what is now 3820 Old

Green Cross Garage (8301 Hamilton Street).

Columbia Pike, and an equal distance up College Avenue and New Cut Road. To the east, the town's jurisdiction stopped at the Patapsco River.

Robert G. Yates Grocery and Florist Shop (8482 Frederick Road), western boundary of Ellicott City's incorporated limits, 1867 to 1935.

Boxcars being unloaded on the Baltimore & Ohio Railroad siding along Maryland Avenue.

Trolley on trestle bridge. Below is the Patapsco Flouring Mill's dam on the Patapsco River. To the far right are the Old Mill Race headgates. circa 1930.

FOUR
1926-1934

Occasionally the hectic pace of responding to alarms throughout Howard County was broken by calls of a more bizarre nature. In May 1926, for instance, the Fire Company was called to answer a fire at a local gasoline station. A newly married couple had stopped to fill the tank of their automobile before heading on their honeymoon. Apparently the station attendant had difficulty determining how much gasoline was actually going into the car's tank, because he lit a match to help him see better. Shortly thereafter the fire engine appeared. By that time, the attendant had discovered that there were safer means of answering his question. No one was injured, but the community enjoyed a chuckle at the expense of the attendant, who also happened to be a member of the Firemen's Association.

In the summer of 1926, the Volunteer Firemen began another reorganization designed to increase the efficiency of their administrative operations. At their annual meeting on June 2, the firemen elected a new captain, selecting G. Ray Helm to replace H. O. Makinson, who had served as captain for the previous two years. The organization also elected Edward D. Hilton as day lieutenant in a unanimous vote, and Charles E. Delosier as night lieutenant in a closely contested election. To guide the Firemen's Association—which theoretically consisted of all the property owners in Howard County—the members chose William F. Kirkwood as president, G. Ray Helm as vice president, Sydney J. Hyatt as secretary, and George W. Carr as treasurer.

Since the residents of the county were not taking as active an interest in the activities of the Association as originally anticipated, President Kirkwood subsequently invited a gathering of Ellicott City businessmen to devise a plan to incorporate the Association and provide advice to help it function as a going concern. According to Dr. Benjamin Mellor Jr., who still served as chief of the Volunteer Firemen, the young men who made up most of the Association's roster felt they needed advice from the older residents of the community, particularly in the area of the Association's financial affairs. "As a unit," explained Chief Mellor, "the firemen felt that they would fare better at the hands of the older committee than at their own hands." Specifically, the firemen feared that they might be criticized for spending the Association's funds unwisely on any purchase they might make. Accordingly, a three-man committee of James Clark, G. Ray Helm, and former Mayor J. Edward Kroh agreed to draw up articles of incorporation and a set of bylaws for the Association. A motion was passed establishing annual dues of twenty-five cents for the Association's members.

If the community seemed unwilling to play an active role in the affairs of the Fire Company, there was no lack of interest in the Association's annual carnival. In fact, by the summer of 1926

the carnival had become a far more elaborate affair than originally envisioned. Once again the firemen staged their carnival on the grounds of the high school (3700 College Avenue), but this time there was such a large crowd for the Wednesday night supper served by the women's committee—chaired by Mrs. B. H. Shipley—that another dinner had to be scheduled for the following night. Furthermore, the affair drew a host of dignitaries, including Governor Albert C. Ritchie, Attorney General Robinson, Congressmen Millard Tydings and Stephen W. Gambrill, plus numerous local political figures. At one point, the crowds grew so large that the town needed to station three special traffic officers to keep automobiles moving. Once again the event grossed nearly $5,000 for the Firemen's Association.

Perhaps because of the increased efficiency of the firefighters, there were fewer major fires in Ellicott City and Howard County in the mid-1920s. "There weren't too many fires," noted B. H. Shipley Jr. in retrospect. "We would go months on end without one. The big problem in the spring and fall would be field and woods fires. And with the steam locomotives on the railroads running up, the sparks from the stack would create a fire hazard."

The only fire that caused extensive

damage in the last six months of 1926 was a blaze that struck several buildings in downtown Lisbon, then the westernmost town in Howard County. On the evening of November 23, a fire broke out in the back of the Dayhoff Garage. Before the engine could arrive from Ellicott City, both the garage and the adjacent Odd Fellows Hall were virtually destroyed. The firefighters had to concentrate their efforts on saving the adjoining buildings. Later, the volunteer firefighters would ask the residents of Lisbon to install a water line to assist in quelling any future blazes.

In an attempt to reduce the threat of fires and personal injuries, Ellicott City officials staged the town's first community fireworks display July 4, 1927. The fireworks were set up in an open field owned by Cabel D. Rogers on Columbia Pike (Old Columbia Pike and Hunt Avenue). The town provided bus service from the Standard Oil Company filling station on Main Street and Columbia Avenue to the site of the festivities. The following year, the display shifted to the former Dundee Summer Hotel, at the corner of Frederick Road and Rogers Avenue (Braebrook). In 1900, this site had been occupied by Mrs. E. E. Baird Chenoweth's Boarding School for Girls. In 1910, it had become the Dundee

Summer Hotel. When local government officials appointed a three-person committee in 1919 to investigate several possible sites for a new school building, two members of the committee—Hart B. Noll and Louis T. Clark—recommended the Dundee property. The third member of the committee, J. Edwin Kroh, favored the Michael Martin property on Columbia Road, (3800 block Old Columbia Pike). When Rock Hill College (3100 College Avenue) burned in 1923, the county officials decided to build the school on that site. The foundation from a stable used by Rock Hill College to accommodate their cattle was utilized to support a house at the intersection of College Avenue and Werner Street (Ross Road).

Since a significant percentage of the fire alarms now involved emergencies outside the limits of Ellicott City, the Volunteer Firemen decided to alter the method of signaling a nighttime fire in the county. Rather than ring the engine house bell and awaken (and produce considerable anxiety among) the residents of the town when a fire occurred in the county, the Firemen's Association installed an electrical system that linked the second engine house, where B. H. Shipley and his family lived, with the homes of ten volunteer firemen, all of whom resided within two hundred yards of the engine house. When Mr. Shipley received an alarm call between 11:30 P.M. and 7:00 A.M., he pressed a button that rang a bell at the bedsides of the firemen, who responded by appearing at the engine house within several minutes, already attired in their turnout gear of protective pants and boots. Fire Department officials believed that this system was the only one of its kind in the state of Maryland at that time.

Officials of the Firemen's Association also hoped that by restricting notice of the fire to the firefighters (for most fires, six or seven volunteers usually responded to an alarm), they might reduce the number of inquisitive telephone calls from curiosity-seekers who still hindered the Fire Company's work. Residents still would be alerted of fires within the limits of Ellicott City by the usual ringing of the bell, which had been relocated to the second firehouse. This eliminated the roundabout procedure of having Mr. Shipley call Charles E. Buetefisch to ring the station bell. Usually Mr. Shipley's son, B. H. Shipley Jr., would ring the bell. "If I wasn't available to ring it," Mr. Shipley recalled, "it would have to wait until my father got there."

At the start of 1927, the Association completed its incorporation plans, reorganizing itself as the Howard County Volunteer Firemen's Association, Inc. The initial members of the Board of Directors were William F. Kirkwood; G. Ray Helm; Dr. Benjamin Mellor Jr.; attorney (and later judge) James Clark; Edward W. Talbott; George W. Carr; Paul G. Stromberg (the editor and subsequently owner of the *Ellicott City Times*); H. Thomas Grimes; Julius A. Kinlein and restaurateur William F. Lilly. At the same time, the Association elected a slate of officers that included Kirkwood (president), Helm (vice president), Carr (treasurer), Elmer C. Cavey (secretary), as well as Fire Chief Mellor and Chief Engineer Shipley.

To ensure that its new members met the standards of the Association, men who wished to join the Volunteer Firemen had to fill out an application form answering health questions such as: "What diseases have you had during the last two years?" "Have you ever received any injury in the head or spine?" "Are you subject to rheumatism?" It also asked about their personal habits: "To what extent, if at all, do you use intoxicating liquor?" "Have you had any scrapes with the law?" "Have you ever been complained of or indicted for or convicted of any violation of the law?" Naturally they also had to promise "to obey all orders issued by the officers in charge pertaining to any fire duties." While new members joined the Association, the oldest active member of the Volunteer Firemen, Mr. Edward D. Hilton, was retired at his own request as an honorary lieutenant.

To augment their newly incorporat-

Second fire house (8316 Main Street) after the 1927 changes and improvements.

ed organization, the Association supervised improvements and an addition—including a hose tower—to the second firehouse, located at 8316 Main Street. Then, in October 1927, the Association's Board of Directors voted to purchase a new chemical engine at a cost of approximately $6,000. The engine, an American LaFrance vehicle, was intended to replace the International engine ("Little Kate") which had been in service since 1925 and which, coincidentally, burned out a bearing just before the new engine arrived. The new engine possessed double the chemical capacity of the International. This was becoming increasingly important as the Fire Company answered more and more

calls from the rural areas of Howard County, where the water supply was frequently insufficient for the primary pumping engine to operate properly. While the firefighters had been forced to ask the County Commissioners for help in purchasing the American LaFrance engine in 1923, this time they were able to pay for the new engine themselves, with the proceeds from the 1926 carnival and the anticipated receipts from the 1927 carnival. "Little Kate," meanwhile, would remain in service as an auxiliary vehicle, used occasionally as a hose wagon to carry extra hose for the pumper.

Before the new chemical engine could arrive, however, Ellicott City suffered one of the worst fires of the decade. On the evening of December 15, 1927, a short circuit in the wiring of a truck parked in the garage of E. A. Talbott (opposite 8386 Court Avenue) started a blaze that spread so rapidly—due to the highly inflammable material in the garage and adjacent stable—that the entire upper end of town was threatened. In fact, a number of Mr. Talbott's neighbors began to gather their belongings and move out of their houses before the Fire Company brought the fire under control. The cold temperatures hampered the firefighters, as did the large crowd of curiosity-seekers—may of whom allegedly came in from nearby rural areas to watch the blaze—who gathered along Main Street. Fortunately, there was virtually no wind to fuel the flames. The Fire Company managed to keep the fire from spreading to Talbott's Lumber and Storage Yard, located next to the garage. One volunteer fireman, Stephen H. Hillsinger, received an injury when he fell into a concrete pit while connecting several sections of fire hose, fracturing his right arm.

No other fires threatened the town for the next several months. In late January 1928, the new American LaFrance chemical engine arrived. Officials of the Firemen's Association immediately put the engine through a series of tests, including a trial run over some of the most challenging hills in Howard County, and claimed afterward that it had performed entirely up to their expectations. The following week, the new engine responded to its first call, an alarm from Jessup. After navigating the nine-mile run in less than fifteen minutes, the engine arrived only to find that the flames had already been extinguished. Nevertheless, the members of the Fire Company told reporters that the engine had run "smooth as a top" en route to the emergency.

Neither the new chemical engine nor the pumper, however, could fight its way through the blizzard that struck Howard County on Saturday, January 28, 1928. Normally, the firemen attached chains to the tires of the fire engines at the first sign of snow (a process that took nearly half an hour to complete), but when the firemen left the engine house on Friday night, the snowstorm had not yet begun. So when an alarm came in at five o'clock Saturday morning, telling the firemen that the cotton mill in Alberton—about five miles away—was on fire, there was no time to mount the chains. Without them, however, the pumper skidded off the road when navigating a turn, and got stuck in a snowbank (2965 Rogers Avenue). Chief Mellor and Charles E. Delosier, who had been driving his own car behind the truck, kept on going to see if they could assist the Alberton Mills Fire Brigade, but by the time they arrived the fire already was under control. Eventually the volunteers managed to get the engine out of the snow bank and brought it back to Ellicott City no worse for the wear.

One of the most bizarre incidents in the history of the Volunteer Firemen of Howard County occurred in April 1928, when the firemen responded to an alarm at the farm of De Wilton C. Parlett, a member of the Howard County Board of County Commissioners. Shortly after 1:00 A.M. on the morning of April 11, Parlett's sister looked out a back window of their Clarksville home and saw that a barn and shed were on fire. Inside the burning buildings were ten cows, eight horses, several prize bulls, over two dozen sheep, and six yearlings, all of whom perished in the blaze before the firefighters could arrive.

Immediately thereafter, another fire appeared at the nearby residence of a farmer named Fedora Boski. When Deputy Sheriff Milton Iglehart and two associates went to Boski's house to warn him of the danger, Boski greeted them with a shotgun and a large butcher knife. Warning them to "get out" and threatening to kill and disembowel anyone who got too close to his house, he proceeded to fire both barrels at the retreating Iglehart and his companions, who prudently withdrew and waited for reinforcements. As police later reconstructed the incident, Boski then set fire to his own house and—while the flames gathered force—shot himself. A charred body, which officials assumed to be Boski, was later found in the cellar of the ruins of his house, which had collapsed about him. Firemen later recalled hearing several gunshots come from inside the house while they waited for Boski to surrender himself and his weapons.

Meanwhile, back at the Parlett estate, the firefighters had hooked the hoses of their pumper to an ice pond and a large water tank on Parlett's property, thereby managing to keep the fire from damaging the commissioner's house. After completing his preliminary investigation, Chief of Police Julius Wosch concluded that Boski—whom Wosch assumed had been suffering from some sort of hallucinations—probably had started the blaze on Parlett's property. It appeared that he had intended to set fire to Parlett's house as well—since a stack of straw was found leaning against the house—before heading back to his own house to take his life.

An analysis of the fire alarms answered by the Volunteer Firemen between September 1927 and July 1928, reveals the changing nature of their work as motorized equipment expanded the effective firefighting range. During that period, the firemen answered seventy-seven alarms, including thirteen chimney fires and another sixteen house fires. They also responded to twenty-nine field or barn fires, indicating their enhanced presence in the rural areas of Howard County. The fact that they answered calls for four auto or truck fires also illustrated the growing number of privately owned automobiles in Howard County during the late 1920s.

Among the more unusual fires which required the firefighters' attention were a blaze on the roof of the Consolidated Gas & Electric Company's power house, two fires in chicken houses, a house fire caused by the owner leaving books on a hot stove, a blaze in a storeroom where egg crates caught fire, and a fire during a funeral process which consumed a hearse and the casket and the body it was carrying.

To show the community's gratitude for the dedication and excellent work of the Firemen's Association, an ad hoc group of Ellicott City residents organized a banquet for the firefighters in January 1929. Held at the Masonic Hall (3825 Church Road), the banquet featured an orchestra, a dinner of roast turkey served by a local women's club, and a host of tributes offered in appreciation of the firemen's service. The entire membership of the Ellicott City Rotary Club, led by club president James Clark, attended the affair, and during the speeches President Clark himself offered his vision of Howard County's future. He said there would be a time when "broad and attractive boulevards would penetrate every corner of the county," facilitating further the firemen's ability to reach any part of Howard County in times of emergency. Among the other speakers was

Howard Travers, the assistant chief of the Baltimore City Fire Department, who commended the work of his Ellicott City brethren and then provided the audience with a series of tips on fire prevention. Dr. Benjamin Mellor Jr. closed the event with a retrospective look at the work of the Ellicott City firemen over the past five years, pointing out the numerous times the men had responded to calls outside Howard County, and praising the foresight of the Howard County Commissioners who had acquired funds to purchase the county's first motorized engine five years earlier. (Ellicott City Town Commissioners paid the interest on the loan that the county received from the Patapsco National Bank.)

Further advances were made in 1929 when the North American Water Works Corporation enhanced Ellicott City's water system. Among the improvements was the installation of two fire hydrants on Court House Hill—one opposite the Emory Methodist Episcopal Church, and the other at the foot of the courthouse steps. Prior to this time, no hydrants had been available in the vicinity of the courthouse, and city officials hoped they would help provide protection for the adjoining section of Main Street.

Then, on April 1, the venerable fire alarm bell that had long hung at the top of the fire engine house at Main Street and Church Road since it was purchased in 1896 was relocated to the new engine house one block further up Main Street. No longer would Charles E. Buetefisch need to run from his home to the engine house on the opposite side of the street to sound the alarm. Obviously officials expected the move to expedite the response of the volunteer firefighters to alarms.

Aside from the work of a firebug who allegedly set several fires on farms in Clarksville in the early spring, the Volunteer Firemen had few serious challenges in 1929 until Howard County suffered one of the worst electrical storms in its history on June 21. The previous week had been extraordinarily warm, and the thunderstorm that put an end to the heat wave also caused numerous fires in the rural areas of the county. The first alarm came in around 11:30 that evening, when the firemen were called to the Atholton area to put out a blaze in a barn that had been struck by lightning. The hay that had been stored in the barn fed the flames so quickly that the barn was almost completely destroyed before firefighters arrived. While they were battling the Atholton fire, another call came in

from a farm in Guilford, where a lightning bolt had set another barn ablaze. This time the chemical engine responded and managed to extinguish the fire before any serious damage occurred. Within the same half-hour, lightning caused yet another blaze. Meanwhile, the torrential rains that accompanied the storm lifted the Patapsco River high above its normal level, creating problems for motorists trying to navigate their way through low-lying areas.

Another fire in late September marked the untimely end of the motorized American LaFrance pumper so recently eulogized by Chief Mellor at the firemen's banquet. On the afternoon of September 19, the attractive three-story estate of Thomas M. Talbott (one of the sons of Edward Alexander Talbott), who lived on Columbia Pike (3864 Old Columbia Pike) just outside the town limits, caught fire. A passing truck driver noticed smoke and flames coming from the roof of the building and alerted the Fire Department. When the firemen arrived with the pumper, they established a hose line running from a nearby stream to the Talbott home. For a time they seemed to be winning the battle, using a steady flow of water to bring the flames under control. Suddenly, however, the engine failed. Sand and pebbles from the sandy stream had been sucked into the pump, disabling it completely. An engine from Catonsville responded to a frenzied call for help, but it, too, could only pump for several minutes at a time, pausing until a dam in the stream could be refilled. When the pumper was taken back to the engine house, Chief Engineer Shipley discovered that the gears had been so badly damaged that it would require $3,000 worth of repairs. Since the engine also needed a new set of tires, along with a fresh coat of paint and varnish, the Department began to seriously entertain the notion of purchasing yet another new pumper.

In December, the Volunteer Firemen's Board of Directors decided to purchase a 1929 American LaFrance "Master Series" pumper costing $12,000. The old engine brought a trade-in allowance of $4,000, thereby defraying the out-of-pocket expenses considerably. Only the second pumper of its type in Maryland, the engine, which featured a six-cylinder, 130 HP motor, reportedly was capable of pumping 750 gallons of water per minute. With an extra-large hose body, it carried approximately 2,200 feet of $2^{1/2}$ inch hose—a necessity in a county where the closest water supply was sometimes 2,000 feet away—and a 28-foot extension ladder. Before actually purchasing the engine, the directors asked representatives of the Underwriters' Association of the Middle Department to inspect and test the pumper. When the experts

The 1929 American LaFrance Pumper, restored to its original condition in 1995. Will be on display in Fire Station No. 2, Montgomery Road and Old Columbia Pike.

expressed their satisfaction with the results, the Association closed the deal. The engine met its first test almost immediately December 27, 1929, when the firemen responded to a fire at the Donaldson School (Trinity School—4985 Ilchester Road), where the nearest supply of water was a swimming pond nearly 1,500 feet away from the fire.

By the end of 1929, the Volunteer Firemen had answered 102 alarms, an increase of thirty over the previous year. In responding to these emergencies, the firemen covered a total of 1,075 miles, including thirty-seven calls of fifteen miles or more, and several runs that took them at least thirty miles. For fires outside the town limits, an average of five firefighters responded, although far more people naturally assisted on fires in Ellicott City itself. The total time expended by the firemen in battling blazes amounted to 167 hours. Property damages due to fire totaled slightly more than $155,000 during the year, although $60,000 resulted from a single blaze in Catonsville, to which the Howard County volunteers responded when a request for assistance from their Baltimore County brethren was received. For most of the alarms, the Fire Company relied on its new chemical engine (Engine Number 3). Few occasions arose requiring the use of more than one engine.

At their regular meeting in the first week of December 1929, the Company elected new officers who were installed in January to serve two-year terms: H. O. Makinson was chosen as captain, aided by Lieutenants Donald L. Brandenburg and William S. Hebb, and Secretary L. Burgess Wamsley. The annual carnival that year had brought the Firemen's Association a net profit of $4,260. The officers planned to use these funds to maintain the Association's existing apparatus and seek new methods of enhancing the efficiency of the firefighting company.

For the next decade, however, additional funds would be difficult to obtain. At the end of October, the nation's stock market plunged in a free fall during several terrifying days which later became known as Black Thursday and Black Tuesday. The Great Crash provided the initial push that sent the U.S. economy into the worst depression in the nation's history. By the winter of 1932–33 the unemployment rate had reached 25 percent, with many cities experiencing jobless rates as high as 60 percent. Everything seemed frozen: banks refused to loan money; businesses began laying off workers; consumers—frightened that they might lose their jobs—stopped buying; and businesses consequently laid off more workers, thus intensifying the horrifying downward spiral. President Herbert Hoover, who refused to take bold initiatives to restore the shattered economy, became the most despised man in America. And there seemed to be no hope in sight.

Howard County did not escape the ravages of the Depression. Unemployment in the area rose sharply. Farm prices, already low throughout the 1920s, suffered even more, and the distress of the farm community increased with the advent of a severe drought in 1930. State officials tried to provide relief through a measure that granted taxpayers additional time to pay their tax bills, but still the economy continued to slide downward.

Like much of the United States during the late 1920s and early 1930s, Howard County also was plagued by widespread violations of the nation's prohibition laws. According to the terms of the Volstead Act, originally passed in 1919, the manufacture, sale, and transportation of intoxicating beverages were declared illegal (although the consumption of liquor remained legal). Prior to that time, Ellicott City had done a significant volume of business in the liquor trade, since the town was the one "wet" spot in an otherwise "dry" Howard County. When prohibi-

tion arrived, the town's four tavern keepers were forced to find different lines of business. One reportedly went into the grocery business, another opened a tobacco shop, and the other two went out of business.

Nevertheless, in March 1930, as part of a sweeping review of county activities, a grand jury presented sixty-five indictments to stem what it considered an outbreak of lawlessness in Howard County. Beyond the cited violations of the Volstead Act, the indictments involved the operation of illegal slot machines, which the grand jury termed a menace to law and order in the county. At the same time, however, the jurors commended the work of the Howard County Fire Department, and praised the Department's excellent relations with county officials and taxpayers.

Numerous small fires kept the firefighters busy in the first few months of the new decade. In a single week in February, the Volunteer Firemen answered five calls, then five more the following week, and another five during a seven-day period in March. Most of the blazes were extinguished with little difficulty. The most worrisome fires were at St. Luke's Congregation on West Main Street, and the Trinity Church on Washington Boulevard in Waterloo. Fortunately, neither fire caused extensive damage.

When spring arrived, the members of the recently formed Ellicott City Rotary Club announced its first major civic project: the beautification of Court House Hill, the rocky and unsightly hillside opposite the courthouse that fronted on Main Street. Ten years earlier, the lot had been purchased by the County Commissioners from the estate of the late Sara Rebecca Talbott, but the commissioners had done nothing to improve the property. By May, the Rotary Club already had sponsored the preliminary steps of the project: a survey of the hill by Guy C. Sykes, the county surveyor who was also a member of the Rotary Club, and the development of a model of the proposed improvement by Baltimore Landscape Architect R. Brooke Maxwell, a native of Howard County.

According to his model, Mr. Maxwell planned to build a set of stone or concrete steps at either end of the lot, starting just behind Main Street. The two pathways would converge about halfway up the hill at "a restful landing." From that point, a single stairway would continue to the top of the hill. In front of the courthouse, Mr. Maxwell intended to construct a park

The Old Mill Race was filled in during the early 1930s by the State Roads Commission using WPA Funds. In the early 1940s an Acme Market was constructed over part of the fill (Frederick Road and Oella Avenue).

with a fountain in the center and seats around the periphery for weary visitors. Besides improving the appearance of the hill, the project also would serve as a memorial to the residents of Howard County who had died in any of the nation's wars, including Confederate soldiers who, in the phrase of the time, "died in defense of a cause consecrated by inheritance as well as sustained by conviction." To commemorate the sacrifice of all these veterans, the Rotary Club planned to set a huge bronze tablet, inscribed with the names of the dead, into the rock face on Main Street.

Estimates of the cost of the beautification project ranged as high as $20,000. Although it received the wholehearted support of the Rotary Club and the endorsement of numerous other civic Associations, the project fell victim to the deleterious effects of the Depression. Most of the club's ambitious plans never reached fruition. "The only thing that ever materialized," explained B. H. Shipley Jr., "was that a fountain was built up in front of the courthouse. The county later sold that property to a lawyer who used it to enlarge his office complex."

Meanwhile, the members of the Volunteer Fire Department were distracted by the eruption of a simmering feud between several officers of the Department and its Board of Directors. According to contemporary news reports, the board refused at its annual meeting in March to approve the elections by the active members of the Department of H. O. Makinson as captain and W. Sears Hebb as lieutenant. The only choice the board endorsed was Donald L. Brandenburg's election as the other lieutenant. After vetoing Makinson and Hebb, the board asked the active members to elect other men in their place. The members of the Department, however, stubbornly refused to change their decision, and once again returned Makinson and Hebb.

While the dispute awaited resolution, the old officers of the Department continued to govern its activities. Meanwhile, Captain Helm—who had lost the recent election to Makinson—brought charges against five members of the Department (Hebb, Brandenburg, L. Burgess Wamsley, Albert Greenwood, and W. Vernon Tittsworth), for allegedly showing disrespect to the Board of Directors and employing language "unbecoming a member of the active department."

To help clear the air, Chief Benjamin Mellor Jr. scheduled a public meeting at the Masonic Hall on the evening of April 3 to hear and discuss the charges. With numerous prominent members of the community in attendance, the meeting ran long into the night. The session finally ended when the Board of Directors and the attorney for the five accused men decided to establish a committee consisting of three members of the board, three active members of the Department, and J. Edwin Kroh (as an impartial referee) to arbitrate the dispute. In the meantime, Helm returned as captain, and Charles E. Delosier and John H. Lyons were elected lieutenants.

After meeting several times, however, the committee reported that it had been unable to make any progress toward "an amicable and easy solution of the entire matter." In returning the matter to the Firemen's Association Board of Directors, the committee strongly urged that the board take whatever steps were necessary "to leave unquestioned the authority reposed in it. The continued success and smooth operation of our department demands that we take a definite stand immediately and, thereby, create a new confidence and respect in constituted authority." Accordingly, at the next meeting of the board on May 15, the resignations of Mr. Greenwood and Mr. Hebb were presented and accepted. One week later, the board heard charges against Mr. Wamsley and Mr. Tittsworth; both men were found guilty and consequently were dismissed from the membership of the active department.

On a more uplifting note, the seventh annual Firemen's Carnival in August 1930 established new records for both attendance and proceeds. Perhaps the presence of Governor Albert C. Ritchie, Congressman Stephen W. Gambrill, and Mayor William F. Broening of Baltimore City helped attract people to the event. Perhaps the promise of an evening of wholesome entertainment allowed Howard County residents to forget the effects of the Depression for at least a few hours. By this time, the carnival had grown into a seven-day affair featuring a baby show, baseball, bingo games, numerous booths offering crafts and food for sale, and a

Mardi Gras on Saturday evening. "The cause is a worthy one," noted the *Ellicott City Times* with approval, "and its unprecedented success will have the effect of greatly encouraging the firemen who give freely and unstintingly of their services both day and night all the year."

If the Depression failed to dampen the enthusiasm of carnival-goers in 1930, the prolonged and devastating drought that summer did create severe problems for the county's firefighters. The fields and brush grew so parched and dry that numerous fires broke out, either through carelessness or accident. During one five-day period in August, the Howard County Fire Department answered alarms for eight separate woods, field, and brush fires in all parts of the county, including a fire on the farm of Guy C. Sykes, one mile west of Ellicott City; another on the Lilly Tyson Ellicott Estate; two woods fires on the same property in Elkridge; and a field fire on a farm on Rogers Avenue, just west of town. To impress the seriousness of the situation upon local residents, a judge convicted and fined a Cooksville man who had carelessly permitted a field fire to get out of control, causing extensive damage to the property of his neighbors.

One of the most devastating fires that hot, dry summer occurred in late August, when a barn and farm machinery were destroyed by a blaze at Folly Quarter Farm, seven miles west of Ellicott City, which had been turned into a novitiate for the Franciscan Fathers. The firefighters responded with two engines, but the blaze—fed by dry hay—had gained too much headway to allow them to save the building. Using water pumped from a branch of the Patuxent River, however, they were able to save the other buildings on the property.

An even more trying situation greeted the firemen in October, when flames cut a wide swath through Jessup in the vicinity of the House of Correction. The blaze spread so quickly that the State Forestry Department called out over five hundred men to battle the fire, along with the Howard County Fire Department, several companies from Baltimore County, and 150 soldiers from nearby Camp Meade. Many of the Ellicott City firefighters spent over six hours battling the flames. Their efforts were constantly frustrated by the changing winds, which would suddenly send the flames blowing back upon the men, surrounding them with burning brush and falling trees. By the time they returned to the engine house, the volunteers—some of whom suffered singed hair and eyebrows from the intense heat—were completely exhausted.

By autumn, the prolonged drought, the numerous fires, and the effects of the Depression seemed to have everyone's nerves on edge in the rural areas of Howard County. The situation required only a spark to send simmering disputes into open violence. In November 1930, the county witnessed a pair of grisly incidents that combined murder, arson, and suicide. On Wednesday, November 12, an elderly farmer named Herman Westphal, who lived on a farm near Atholton, shot and killed Charles Hubbel, a farm laborer who lived with his brother, also in the Atholton area. The two men had long been enemies, largely because Westphal's former wife, who had left him several years earlier, had subsequently married Hubbel. The young lady in question, whose maiden name was Gussie Dreislein, had married Westphal when she was only sixteen; he was several decades older. After bearing him one child, she left Westphal, claiming that he had beaten her. Three years later, Gussie obtained a divorce and married Hubbel, who worked at numerous farms around Atholton.

As police reconstructed the scene, Westphal and Hubbel had been hunting together on the afternoon of November 11. Upon returning to Westphal's house, Westphal apparently killed Hubbel with a shotgun blast to the head. It seems he then set fire to his house, possibly to disguise his crime, and retreated to a barn outside. When Police Chief Wosch arrived, Westphal was lying on a pile of hay with a bullet wound in his left side and a revolver on the ground nearby. Although he claimed that Hubbel had shot him in a duel, authorities suspected that Westphal had inflicted the wound himself. Westphal was taken to University Hospital in Baltimore. The following day, a coroner's jury charged him with Hubbel's murder.

Two weeks later, firefighters were called to the scene of another murder, this time in the rural community of Alpha. On Saturday, November 22, a call came into the Ellicott City engine house alerting the Fire Department to a blaze at the farm of Robert T. Shipley. When the men arrived, they discovered the farmhouse in flames. Chief Engineer Shipley led his men into the house, entering through the second floor and making their way down to the first level. There the smoke was so thick that Chief Engineer Shipley had to crawl about on his hands and knees, searching for survivors. On the floor

outside the dining room, Chief Engineer Shipley discovered the body of Mrs. Georgia Shipley, the farmer's wife, her clothes afire. Slapping out the flames with his hands, Chief Engineer Shipley then had to feel his way toward an escape route out of the burning room. After trying to search other rooms of the house, the firefighters had to retreat before the rising flames.

Despite Chief Engineer Shipley's heroics, the woman was, unfortunately already dead, the victim of a gunshot wound. Several hours later, authorities discovered the lifeless body of her estranged husband, Robert T. Shipley, in the loft of their barn. The couple had a long history of marital quarrels, and their teenaged daughter later told investigators that she had heard them arguing earlier that day. In fact, her father had ordered her out of the house. Shortly thereafter, she had heard the sound of a gunshot. Coroner Frank C. Higinbothom subsequently returned a verdict of murder and suicide, claiming that Robert T. Shipley had shot and killed his wife, then set fire to the house, and finally shot himself with a .32 caliber revolver, which was found lying near his body in the barn. Ironically, the barn in which Robert T. Shipley died was the same place where his father-in-law had been found hanged in 1912.

As if these appalling incidents were not enough, the Volunteer Firemen had to battle a series of field and house fires in the area between Ellicott City and Washington Boulevard in November and December. The frequency of fires in the same vicinity made fire and police officials suspicious. In the first week of December, authorities arrested a fifteen-year-old youth from Virginia who was living with a friend on Montgomery Road in Elkridge. Following his arrest, the young man confessed to setting a number of houses afire because he "liked to see fires." He was subsequently tried for arson.

Partly because of the extended drought, the yearly statistics for the Fire Department for 1930 showed a significant increase over the number of alarms the preceding year. In all, the Howard County Volunteer Firemen responded to 164 alarms, up from 102 in 1929. Sixty-five of the fires originated in fields or woods; another twenty-three in out-buildings; and fifty-five fires started in private dwellings. The total distance traveled by the firefighters in response to alarms—1,850 miles—was only slightly greater than the previous year. For most of the calls, the firemen used only Engine Number 3, the chemical engine. In fact, the large pumper was

called into service on only a few occasions. Perhaps the most remarkable statistic—and the greatest tribute to the efficiency of the firefighters—was the fact that in none of the emergencies during that difficult year did a fire spread beyond the building in which it started.

Ellicott City was then in the midst of a remarkable stretch of eight years during which time there were no major fires—that is, fires resulting in a loss of $100 or more in property damage—within the town itself. As Chief Engineer Shipley pointed out, this probably represented a record. It may not have been a coincidence that this eight-year period began with the purchase of the Fire Company's new pumper in 1924, although the Fire Company's concerted efforts to educate the public on the importance of fire prevention also played a significant role in the absence of serious fires. The only major conflagration that occurred between 1930 and 1933 in all of Howard County was a fire at the property of Flora Bower Harrison in Patapsco Heights (3540 Church Road) on August 2, 1932. At the time, the general area between the Patapsco Female Institute and Linwood (Church Road and Park Drive) was known as Patapsco Heights, and the roadway as Merrick's Lane (Church Road). Ms.

Harrison's home, a fifteen-room unoccupied frame dwelling known as "El Dorado," was completely destroyed. Unfortunately, while the volunteer firemen were battling the blaze, one firefighter was injured.

During 1932, the Howard County Volunteer Firemen's Association responded to a total of 120 alarms, traveling over fifteen hundred miles to answer calls. Most of the fires occurred in houses, chimneys, or outbuildings, although the eight "blazing auto" alarms that year indicated a growing population of automobile owners in the county. An average of nine firefighters responded to each alarm, and although some fires were disposed of within minutes, there was one blaze—a fire in a large pile of slab wood on a farm in Dayton—that took four and a half hours to quell.

In the winter of 1933, the nation entered the worst period of the Great Depression. Banks closed by the score as depositors panicked and the American people sank into a dangerous mood of despair and, in some cases, anger. The year began badly in Howard County, too, as a fire in late January 1933 completely destroyed a barn on the farm of State's Attorney James Clark at Elioak. Two weeks later, one of the Fire Company's engines—the light chemical truck ("Little Kate") constructed out of a secondhand motor and chassis in 1926 by Chief Engineer Shipley and several of his colleagues—was wrecked while responding to an alarm in Ilchester. As it was heading east on Main Street in Ellicott City, the chemical truck was crowded by a careless westbound car. As it skidded on the ice-covered street, the truck veered out of control and collided with several automobiles parked on the south side of Main Street. Although none of the six firemen on the truck were injured, the engine was totally wrecked and had to be dismantled. Meanwhile, the blaze in Ilchester was put out by the Volunteer Fire Company, with help from their Catonsville brethren and the use of a portable pump that allowed them to use water from a stream about one thousand feet away from the burning building.

The worst fire of 1933 in Howard County occurred February 22, when twenty firefighters were called out to battle a blaze on the property of Mrs. Thaddeus Grimes in Patapsco Heights (3611 Church Road). The fire began in the Grimes barn, then spread to several adjoining outbuildings. By using the American LaFrance pumper, which drafted about eight thousand gallons of water from the Grimes well, and their portable pumps—which they attached to several neighborhood pumps—the firemen managed to contain the fire. One of the firefighters, Mr. Charles P. Ditch, suffered painful burns to his face, head, and hands, and had to seek medical treatment. (Mr. Ditch's devotion to duty, however, led him to stay on the job for three hours after being burned, before he agreed to see a doctor.)

In the summer of 1933, the community of Woodbine, in the western part of Howard County, experienced a series of frightening fires that threatened to wipe out most of the community's entire business district. In the early morning hours of Sunday, June 25, a fire broke out in a private garage and then spread to the Woodbine Canning Factory, a blacksmith shop, a grain elevator, a private home, a general store, and a variety of outbuildings. The Mount Airy Fire Company realized at the outset that they could not control the fire alone, but because the telephones in Woodbine were out of order at the time, the volunteers had to go to Lisbon to call the Ellicott City firefighters for assistance. In the meantime, the fire gathered considerable momentum. By the time the Howard County Volunteer

Ellicott City Active Volunteer Firemen with the 1929 Engine on the left and the 1928 Engine on the right—June, 1934.

Firemen arrived, the flames already had destroyed the garage—including eleven automobiles stored there—and almost half of the canning factory. Ellicott City firefighters, standing on stacks of wooden cases of canned peas as they held the hose line fighting the fire, could hear and feel the explosion of cans under their feet.

It took almost five hours for the firefighters to bring the fire under control; fortunately, they were able to use the American LaFrance pumper to pump water out of the Patapsco River to quell the blaze. The following week, another fire broke out in a private home in Woodbine. At the time of the dwelling fire, three volunteers of the Ellicott City Fire Department were in Woodbine, looking over the damage done in the previous fire. Again the alarm was sent to Ellicott City, although this time the volunteers arrived in time to keep the fire from spreading.

Later that summer, the volunteer firemen's annual carnival—the tenth since the event began in 1924—celebrated another tremendous success, setting new attendance marks as more than ten thousand people crowded onto the grounds on the final night alone. "Traffic was literally tied up on Main Street for three hours, cars were turned away from the carnival's parking grounds, and many left their cars in Baltimore County," testified one impressed onlooker. "Main Street was filled with cars whose owners were at the carnival. There was a line of parked autos extending up College Avenue to the entrance of Patapsco Manor Sanitarium (4110 College Avenue) and out New Cut Road beyond the 'Forty Acres.' "

But the carnival was not the only event that brought together the volunteer firemen and the community. Beginning in the mid-1930s, the Howard County Volunteer Firemen's Association intensified its efforts to educate the public on such topics as fire prevention and the lifesaving services the volunteer firemen could provide. In August 1933, for instance, the Fire Company reminded the county's residents (via the pages of the *Ellicott City Times*) that they should call the firemen as soon as possible whenever someone was in danger of drowning. "Several times the Ellicott City Fire Department has answered calls for lifesaving apparatus [a Mine Safety Appliance Company Type 'O' Inhalator—currently on display at the Firehouse Museum, 3829 Church Road] to assist in reviving persons who had been near death from drowning," the notice said, but "the calls really came too late." In one tragic case, nearly an hour elapsed after a youth had been pulled from the water before the firemen were called to bring their resuscitation equipment. (In the 1930s, the Ellicott City Fire Department was the only fire department outside the city of Baltimore to have an inhalator.)

In October, the Volunteer Firemen's Association joined Governor Ritchie in celebrating Fire Prevention Week. As part of the program, the volunteer firefighters arranged an exhibit to help educate the public in methods of stopping fires before they got started, and urged local ministers to stress the theme of fire prevention to their congregations during their weekly worship services.

During these years, the Volunteer Firemen's Association also stepped up its efforts to educate its own members on modern firefighting and lifesaving techniques. In 1933, the firemen heard lectures from the chairman of the Maryland State Firemen's Association Committee on Fire Inspection and Fire Prevention; the chief of the Baltimore City Fire Department; a representative of the Baltimore City Bureau of Building (who spoke on electrical hazards); and a first aid instructor from the Baltimore City Fire Department. Numerous members of the Department also attended standard and advanced

courses in first aid by the American Red Cross and the Baltimore City Fire Department, as well as demonstrations of the latest equipment by representatives of firefighting apparatus companies. Perhaps most importantly, five members of the Volunteer Fire Company—B. H. Shipley Jr., John C. Kirkwood, C. Edwin Wallenhorst, Albert H. Laumann, and Francis J. Otten Jr.—attended the Maryland State Firemen's Association's short course at the recently established Fire College at the University of Maryland. The Fire College, which had first offered courses in 1930, was an intensive, three-day training program conducted through the auspices of the Fire Service Extension Department of the College of Engineering. It proved immediately successful, and the Howard County Volunteer Firemen's Association was one of the first groups of firefighters in the state to take advantage of the college's offerings.

Public education and advanced training could enhance firefighting efforts within the county, but the decades-old problem of the lack of an adequate supply of water—a problem exacerbated by the recent demise of the chemical engine—still bedeviled Howard County firefighters. Two fires at the end of 1933 illustrated this dilemma dramatically. On the evening of November 30, a fire destroyed a large barn on a Lisbon farm, causing more than $10,000 damage. Although the Fire Company responded quickly to the alarm, they had to lay a line of hose nearly 2,500 feet to the nearest stream. By the time they were able to start pumping water, the flames already had consumed most of the building.

Then, on the afternoon of December 11, a fire destroyed a series of buildings on an Ilchester estate about four miles southeast of Ellicott City. The strong winds that raged that day carried the flames from a tenant house to the larger main house on the property (which stood on one of the highest hills in the county), and subsequently carried blazing shingles to a barn nearly half a mile away, setting it, too, on fire. Thence the wind carried cinders to an outbuilding on the estate of Misses Virginia and Antoinette Pindell, two retired teachers who lived nearby. All those structures were destroyed, and numerous trees in the line of the fire suffered damage, but the Fire Company finally managed to bring the blaze under control. Even with the gale-force winds, however, the firefighters were convinced they would have been able to save more of the buildings if there had been an adequate source of water nearby.

Fifteen months later, another fire would strike the Pindell property (4800 block of Ilchester Road), with tragic consequences. During the early morning of March 13, 1935, a fire broke out on the rear porch of the Pindell sisters' two-story home. A servant who lived at the house awoke to find smoke pouring out of the kitchen. He ran upstairs and roused the two elderly women, who managed to flee the house with only minor injuries. As the young man ran to a nearby farm to telephone the Fire Company in Ellicott City, one of the sisters—Antoinette Pindell—ran back into the house to recover $100 in cash she had withdrawn from the bank earlier that day. She never returned. Overcome by smoke, she collapsed just inside the front door. Without any source of water in the vicinity, the firefighters were unable to save the house, which was more than one hundred years old. When B. H. Shipley finally entered the smoldering building, he discovered Miss Pindell's body lying in the front hallway, with scraps of her charred pocketbook beside her.

*The property of J. W. Hillsinger, Loretta J. Hillsinger, Edward
W. and Sallie E. Talbott (8267 Main Street) was selected
December 2, 1937, as the site for the new Ellicott City Post
Office. Sale to the United States of America was finalized
January 4, 1939.*

FIVE
1934-1941

As the Howard County Volunteer Firemen's Association headed into 1934, it continued to expand its services to the public as it evolved into a modern firefighting organization. During 1934, Dr. Benjamin Mellor Jr. stepped down as chief after decades of dedicated service to Ellicott City and Howard County. He was replaced by B. H. Shipley, who recently had been honored by the members of the Fire Company with a gold token of appreciation for his own years of service. To assist Chief Shipley, the Association elected George W. Carr president, J. Edwin Kroh vice president, Elmer C. Cavey secretary, and Thomas E. Brian treasurer. Charles P. Ditch was named captain, aided by Lieutenants Robert E. Hood and Edwin A. Miller, and assistant engineer Frank K. Collette. In addition, there were thirty-one active members of the Association, and three active reserve officers (Captain G. Ray Helm, Lieutenant Edward D. Hilton, and Lieutenant Charles E. Delosier).

Shortly after assuming his post as chief, Mr. Shipley inaugurated a series of messages to the public which were designed to heighten residents' awareness of fire dangers. During the Christmas season of 1934, he issued a statement urging them to exercise caution in the purchase of holiday lights and illuminated displays. "Don't use candles or other open flame lights on or near the tree," Chief Shipley reminded county residents. "Don't use paper or other inflammable material around electric lights for decorations. Don't be careless in smoking or lighting matches near the tree. Don't leave the tree in a heated room too long, for it dries quickly and becomes very dangerous. Above all, don't regard these suggestions as something to be forgotten. They are important. Be careful and be happy."

In a similar vein, Chief Shipley issued another statement at the end of June 1935, informing Howard Countians that Fourth of July fireworks caused nearly one million dollars in fire damage each year. "In addition to the fires due to fireworks and matches igniting clothing and causing death and severe burns," he wrote, "Fire Departments have to face the problems of a large number of other fires . . . caused by fireworks igniting wooden shingle roofs and other readily combustible materials in the community."

Canteen served during training evolutions by Ladies Auxiliary.

Meanwhile, the Firemen's Association had started to enter a variety of Fire Company parades and firefighting competitions throughout the region, often finishing first (during one stretch in 1936, the Company won eight straight first-place awards for best appearance), or winning at least honorable mention awards. The Association also launched a series of junior first aid classes designed to teach the basics of first aid to young men between the ages of twelve and seventeen.

As the Association expanded its efforts beyond the actual fighting of fires, they received valuable assistance from a new local organization that came into existence at the end of 1934. There still were no women firefighters in Howard County—the first female mem-

The 1964 International Travelall purchased with funds donated by the Ladies Auxiliary to the Ellicott City Volunteer Firemen's Association.

ber of the Volunteer Firemen's Association would not be admitted for several decades—but in October 1934 a group of ladies who wanted to demonstrate their support for the Association in tangible ways met to organize the Ladies' Auxiliary to the Howard County Volunteer Firemen's Association. (They were encouraged in this venture by the Ladies' Auxiliary to the Maryland State Firemen's Association, which had been created in 1932.) Gathering initially on the evening of October 2 at the Howard County Courthouse, the Ladies' Auxiliary elected a slate of officers that included Mrs. B. H. Shipley as president, Mrs. George Ogle as vice president, Mrs. G. Ray Helm as secretary, and Miss E. Clare Fells as treasurer. According to the articles of the organization, membership in the Ladies' Auxiliary was open to "any lady in good standing," and members were expected to pay dues of ten cents per month. The object of the Ladies' Auxiliary was "to cooperate with and assist the Fire Company socially and financially."

In the years to come, the Ladies' Auxiliary would fulfill that purpose and more. For the first several years of its existence, the organization helped the firefighters by hosting dinners for the active members of the Fire Department, holding Christmas parties for the firemen and their wives, and presenting the firemen with useful gifts or funds to help defray the cost of new equipment. The Ladies' Auxiliary quickly expanded its activities by sponsoring a wide variety of bake sales, bazaars, dances, dinners, raffles, and rummage sales. During flower festivals and art shows in Ellicott City, they would frequently operate food stands to raise additional funds. To boost morale and visibility within the community, the Ladies' Auxiliary also organized a drill team which participated in parades throughout the state, bringing home numerous trophies and prizes. And to strengthen their ties with their sisters in other towns, the group joined the Ladies' Auxiliary to the Maryland State Firemen's Association in May 1935, sending a pair of delegates to the state organization's annual convention, where they could share ideas and concerns.

By 1935, the nation had begun to emerge from the Great Depression under the leadership of President Franklin Delano Roosevelt, although full recovery still lay six years into the future. During the spring of that year, the Howard County Volunteer Firemen's Association used a portion of the funds it had raised from its successful annual carnivals to purchase a new American LaFrance "Scout" triple combination pumping engine. Capable of pumping five hundred gallons of water

per minute, the "Scout"—which came to be known as Engine Number 4—cost $5,700, and was placed into service April 4.

To further enhance the safety and efficiency of the county's firefighting efforts, the Fire Department installed a pair of traffic sirens along Main Street in Ellicott City in June 1935. The sirens—which had been purchased for the department by the Ellicott City Town Commissioners shortly before the town lost its incorporated status—had become necessary as a result of increasing automobile traffic within the town.

The late State Senator Joseph L. Donovan, at the request of the general public, introduced a bill to the General Assembly of Maryland to revoke the Certificate of Charter for Ellicott City. This legislation was approved with the effective date of July 1, 1935.

Due to the location of the firehouse at a curve in the road, motorists had experienced difficulty seeing or hearing the engines before they pulled out of the firehouse. There had been numerous times when cars had nearly collided with one of the fire trucks. With one siren located at the intersection of Fel's Lane and Main Street, and the other opposite the Ellicott City Garage (8289 Main Street), the city hoped to provide adequate warning to drivers. According to a Fire Department spokesman, the sirens would be used only between the hours of 6:00 A.M. and midnight, thereby alleviating residents' concerns of wailing sirens in the middle of the night. But there was no question as to which vehicle had the right of way when the alarms sounded. "When hearing the sirens," advised Chief Shipley, "motorists should pull to the side and stop until the apparatus has passed, thus preventing accidents and the loss of both life and valuable fire equipment."

Such communications with the public became a hallmark of Chief Shipley during his years at the helm of the Howard County Fire Department. More than any of his predecessors, Chief Shipley actively sought to educate county residents about the work of the Department, and the many ways in which they could help prevent fires. Often Chief Shipley turned a destructive fire into an educational experience for local citizens, using it to teach them how to avoid similar conflagrations in the future.

One such event occurred in the summer of 1935, when the county suffered a series of fires that seemed to have started spontaneously in piles of stored hay and grain. Speaking to the county's farmers, Chief Shipley warned them that "the percentage of moisture contained in hay and unthrashed grain this year" represented a significant fire hazard during spells of hot weather. "I advise farmers of this county who have their barns and barracks stored with the above to make a thorough inspection of the buildings at least once a day for excessive heat or a steaming condition," concluded Chief Shipley.

To all the citizens of Howard County, Chief Shipley issued a series of messages that were published in the *Ellicott City Times* in September and early October 1935 entitled "You and Your Fire Department." Designed to heighten public awareness of fire safety in the days leading up to Fire Prevention Week, Chief Shipley's notices went far toward convincing local residents that they could prevent many, if not most of the fires that struck Howard County. Reminding his readers that "the safety of the lives of the loved ones in your home and the security of your property depends largely upon how well you and the Fire Department cooperate." Chief Shipley pointed out that most fires "start from known hazards, which may be eliminated easily or safeguarded by a little serious consideration and care on the part of each of us."

Accordingly, he recommended periodic inspections of home furnaces and stoves, the use of proper wiring techniques, adherence to modern building codes, and the use of fire resistant materials in housing construction. Citizens would need to devote some of their free time to educating themselves further on fire prevention, Chief Shipley conceded, but in return for "this small expenditure of time," they would "receive knowledge that may be the means of saving property from destruction and loved ones from violent death."

It was especially important for women to learn more about fire prevention, Chief Shipley added, since many fires began in the home, and since the probability of survival during a fire was considerably less for women than for men. Hundreds of women perished each year in fires that started through experiments in "home dry cleaning," when homemakers tried to use a highly explosive liquid as a cleaning agent. All too often, women tried to add kerosene into a stove that was already hot, thereby producing a dangerous explosion. The upsurge in the number of women who smoked cigarettes also increased the hazards of fire, due to the careless use of matches and discarded cigarettes. "The significant thing to be remembered by all women," concluded Chief Shipley, "is that most fire deaths occur before the fire apparatus arrives on the scene. The only possible way to prevent these tragedies is through education. Every women's organization should have fire safety as a definite project somewhere in its program."

Chief Shipley's messages were seconded—with appropriate quotations from scripture—by community spokesmen, including Reverend E. A. Godsey, the minister of the Bethany Methodist Episcopal Church (2875 Bethany Lane). In early May 1936, a fire threatened to destroy the entire church, but the prompt arrival of the volunteer firemen managed to preserve the venerable structure. "The availability of firefighting apparatus and firefighting volunteers are factors which the average citizen or group find easy to take for granted," noted Reverend Godsey. "But 'when your own house is on fire' how tremendously important they become! Since 'no man knoweth the day nor the hour' when he may need their services, it does seem to me the epitome of wisdom and decency to commend them for their work and pledge ourselves to cooperate with them in the effort of maintaining and extending the services of fire protection in our community."

Toward that end, the Fire Department installed two new fire hydrants along Main Street in Ellicott City in May 1936. One of the hydrants was located at the intersection of

Columbia Road and Main Street, while the other was placed directly across from the fire engine house. Both mains were six inches in diameter and possessed the capability of flowing 750 gallons of water per minute, nearly double the capacity of the old hydrants. Several months later, another four-inch water main and fire hydrant was installed on Hill Street, providing additional protection for the residents of that part of town.

Chief Shipley's public education campaign seemed to be having the desired effect. In 1936, the Howard County Volunteer Firemen's Association was called on to answer only a total of 105 alarms, including 27 dwelling fires and 22 chimney fires. Most of these fires were relatively minor affairs; the average time spent pumping water to fight each fire was only 21 minutes. Clearly most of the fires occurred outside the Ellicott City limits, since the average distance traveled answering each alarm was 10.5 miles. The only fatality that year resulted from a one-car automobile accident. One disturbing note in the Association's annual report was the fact that an average of only five volunteers turned out to answer an alarm. While this statistic may have resulted from the relatively trivial nature of most of the fires, it also may have reflected an increasing unwillingness on the part of local employers to allow volunteer firemen to leave their jobs to respond to alarms during the daytime.

For 1937, the Association elected Dr. Louis L. Brown president. Naturally Chief Shipley retained his post, but now he was seconded by his son, B. H. Shipley Jr., as captain. The younger Shipley, who was usually known as "Harrison" to distinguish him from his father (who was called "Harry"), was twenty-two years old at the start of 1937. He had been an active member of the Volunteer Firemen's Association since 1930. Following his graduation from Ellicott City High School, he had attended St. John's College in Annapolis for two years, and then went to work for a series of New Deal agencies, including the Civil Works Administration, the Public Works Administration, and the Works Progress Administration. In 1936 he had accepted a job in the shipping department of the Carey Machinery & Supply Company in Baltimore; by 1937 he had already advanced into the billing department. As captain of the Howard County Volunteer Firemen's Association, B. H. Shipley Jr. was responsible for assisting the chief in planning, training, and educating the public on fire prevention, and coordinating and supervising the operation of fire suppression.

Chief Shipley would need a capable captain more than ever in 1937, for he took on additional responsibilities himself when he was elected president of the Maryland State Firemen's Association at the organization's annual convention in June. Mr. Shipley had, in fact, been a candidate for the presidency the previous year as well, but had stepped aside in favor of another candidate, J. Millard Tawes, who went on to become governor of Maryland several decades later. For the previous several years, Chief Shipley's involvement with the State Association—which represented 160 local volunteer companies—had been steadily growing, as he accepted a one-year term as a member of its executive committee, and a three-year term on the State Fire Prevention and Inspection Committee.

As president of the Maryland State Firemen's Association, Chief Shipley urged his brother firefighters to conduct the same sort of extensive public education campaigns on fire prevention that he had been waging in Howard County. Chief Shipley also oversaw the inauguration of a firemen's training course that could be taught on the local level, to supplement the short course offered at College Park. In 1937, the General Assembly appropriated funds to assist the University of Maryland Department of Vocational Education in organizing and coordinating this course as university extension work. The course itself was outlined at a conference of the Fire College Committee, which included Chief Shipley, Dean Steinberg of the university's School of Engineering, and Professor R. B. Criswell, also a member of the School of Engineering. By the summer of 1938, fifty percent of the local companies across the state had men attending the course at regional centers, a far greater number than ever attended the university's short course.

Designed to increase the efficiency of firefighters by systematizing training procedures, encouraging cooperation, and teaching firemen to "learn to fight fires with your brains, not just your brawn," the forty-hour course consisted of thirteen two-hour indoor classes—with lesson material furnished by the University of Maryland—on such topics as "Attack, Control and Extinguishment," "Salvage and Ventilation," "First Aid and Rescue," and "Chemical Extinguishers," supplemented by another ten hours of outside drill with all types of apparatus and equipment available. After passing a series of quizzes and tests, the firemen would receive award cards attesting to their completion of the course; more importantly, they would have the confidence and knowledge that they had improved their own capability to fight fires in the most safe and effective manner.

Not surprisingly, the Howard County Fire Department decided to offer the fire service extension course at the engine house on the Association's regular meeting nights. Captain B. H. Shipley Jr. served as the instructor, and fifteen active members—including his dad, Chief Shipley—signed up to take the course that year.

Quilt top presented to B. H. Shipley at the 1938 Maryland State Firemen's Association Convention. Hand quilted in 1996.

When his year-long tenure as president of the Maryland State Volunteer Firemen's Association ended in 1938, Chief Shipley received a special gift. At the annual convention each year, the outgoing president of the State Association was presented with a quilt top fashioned by Mrs. Emma Farrell of Laurel, Maryland. After Chief Shipley was presented with the quilt top, the Ladies' Auxiliary to the Howard County Volunteer Firemen's Association invited Mrs. Farrell to come and speak to their organization in October 1938, which she graciously consented to do. The quilt top was put together, hand-quilted, and completed by Mrs. Betty Jane Klima of Ocean City, Maryland, in 1996.

As Chief Shipley and the officers of the Howard County Volunteer Firemen's Association continued to promote the causes of modern, advanced training techniques and fire prevention education, the Association also decided that the Fire Department required an improved physical plant. Over the past decade, the demands on the Department had been steadily growing, and even though it had spent over $50,000 on apparatus, the cramped, antiquated firehouse itself had become increasingly inadequate for the Department's needs. At the annual meeting of the Association's Board of Directors in January 1937, the board decided to embark upon a preliminary investigation of the cost of new facilities.

After an architect had designed a suitable plan that seemed to fulfill the Department's present and future needs, the Board of Directors presented the proposal to the Board of County Commissioners, who approved the plan. The proposal was contingent upon the acquisition of a federal grant from the Public Works Administration; unfortunately, the PWA's annual funds ran out shortly after the county submitted its proposal. The following year, however, PWA officials granted the county's request and agreed to furnish 45 percent of the total cost of construction, which was estimated at approximately $35,000. In return, the county consented to pick up the tab for the remainder of the building.

For its part, the Firemen's Association purchased and paid cash for a suitable lot—namely, the property owned by Mary Rebecca Makinson, Lot 52 (8390 Main Street), formerly part of the tract known as "Mount Misery"—just west of the previous firehouse location. The Association also agreed to waive the county's annual payment for maintenance of the Fire Department (an amount that ranged between $1,000 and $1,500), so that amount could be used to amortize the bonds sold to finance the construction. The combination of federal financing and the Association's decision to waive its annual payments meant that the cost to the county's taxpayers would be minimal. As the Association's president, Dr. Louis L. Brown reminded the county's residents they were still receiving top-quality fire protection at a relatively slight cost. "If Howard County was obliged to buy fire apparatus and maintain a paid department," noted Dr. Brown, "a great difference would be noticed by the taxpayer."

To show their appreciation for the volunteer firefighters, and to enjoy a good time, Brown suggested that the county residents give their usual support to the Association's annual carnival. As usual, the 1937 carnival was held on the grounds of Ellicott City High School (3700 College Avenue).

The high school's campus was large enough to host the carnival, but the school's baseball games were still held on a separate forty-acre lot about a half-mile away (3940 New Cut Road). The lot known as "Forty Acres" had formerly served the same purpose for the students of Rock Hill College.

In 1913, Herman "Babe" Ruth, a member of the St. Mary's Industrial School, played baseball in Ellicott City against a team from Rock Hill College.

This was prior to signing with Jack Dunn of the Baltimore Orioles February 14, 1914. On October 17, 1914, Babe Ruth was married to Helen Woodford in Ellicott City at St. Paul's Catholic Church.

Forty Acres was an extraordinarily popular location for sporting events, serving as the site of the Howard County Board of Education's annual county-wide track and field day ("Rally Day"), and numerous games featuring Ellicott City's amateur baseball and football teams. In 1937, several games of the Maryland State Amateur Baseball championship were held on the field. That year the Ellicott City Hoplites of the Southwestern County League won the championship by defeating the Paramount Club of the Belair Road League September 8, 1937, at Old Oriole Park on Greenmount Avenue and 29th Street in Baltimore.

In addition, there was a gymnasium on the high school's lot (used by both the school and the Hoplites' basketball team). A swimming pool was located on Forty Acres for the use of the general public. Athletes or spectators who needed a refreshing drink during a contest could avail themselves of the steady stream of cool water that flowed from a spring through a pipe inserted in the hillside of the property. Indeed, some

Ellicott City Hoplites, amateur baseball team.

local residents made regular trips to the hillside with their own containers to bottle the water and take it home.

As the population of Howard County grew, it became increasingly clear that the county required more than one fire company. In 1937, the Savage Volunteer Fire Company was organized to provide service to the southeastern part of the county. The establishment of the Savage Company required the two companies to coordinate their activities, of course, and officials of both companies maintained close telephone contact to provide the maximum level of protection.

In the spring of 1938, the Board of Directors of the Howard County Volunteer Firemen's Association received the first complaint in the fourteen years of the Fire Department's existence. The difficulties stemmed from the decision by the Board of Directors not to respond to the many field fires that plagued the rural sections of Howard County unless buildings were endangered. Although this decision was made reluctantly, it reflected a consensus from active members of the Fire Department who had grown weary of battling fires set by property owners who neglected to take the proper precautions to control the flames.

Furthermore, local employers of volunteer firemen informed the Association's directors that they thought it unfair to expect them to pay the firefighters their wages when they were constantly having to leave their jobs to fight field fires that were the result of negligence. As a result, the board decided that it "could not order our men to fight field fires without endangering the efficiency of our Department," and it passed a resolution instructing the active members of the Association "not to fight field fires; but, if they received a call saying that buildings are in danger, they were to answer the call . . . and if there was any danger of fire reaching any building, they were to stand by for emergency but were not to fight field fires unless this emergency occurred."

Between the time the board voted and the publication of the decision in the *Ellicott City Times*, a dispute occurred between volunteer firemen and several county residents who had, in fact, started a brush fire that got out of control. The dispute was over the fact that the Ellicott City firefighters would not take their two-wheel drive chemical engine out into a plowed field to attempt to extinguish a hollow tree fire. There were no close exposures; in fact, the fields nearby were already burnt over. When the firemen refused to quell the blaze, even after the property owners offered to pay them for their services, the residents became enraged and registered a very vocal complaint. The board responded by explaining its decision to the public and assuring everyone that "our men will still continue to give efficient service in our County at any time, day or night, when they are called upon to fight any fire which endangers any building or lives."

At the same time, Chief Shipley recommended that certain measures be taken to

Howard County Police Headquarters and Trial Magistrate Court 1939–1964 (8316 Main Street). Former second firehouse.

Route 40 bridge completed in June 1937 over the Patapsco River. Material and supplies to do the construction were moved to the site via a corduroy road that extended from Church Road Extended (Park Drive) to the State Park and was built by the Civilian Conservation Corps (CCC) workers. A rail siding was installed west of the Hollifield Tunnel to move in the construction equipment, circa 1937

works. Since similar laws reportedly had enjoyed substantial success in protecting life and property throughout Maryland, Chief Shipley deemed it "of the utmost importance that a law of this type be passed as soon as possible."

In March 1939, a fire that nearly got out of control in the lower end of Ellicott City illustrated once again the inadequacy of the town's water system. A fire broke out in a barn on College Avenue, southeast from Main Street, and when the firefighters arrived and hooked up a hose to the nearest hydrant, they found that they could not get even a trickle of water. The usual procedure in this part of town—which was served by a two-inch line that terminated (3943 College Avenue)—was to first shut off the water supply of the Doughnut Corporation of America, across the Patapsco River. But this time, even shutting off the line to DCA did not provide an adequate water supply, and the barn burned completely to the ground. Fortunately, the two fire engines carried tanks—holding one hundred gallons and two hundred gallons of water, respectively—that the firefighters used to keep a nearby house from also going up in flames.

For the Volunteer Firemen's

diminish the possibility of serious fires in Howard County. Specifically, he urged the Board of County Commissioners to instruct the county's police force to enforce rigidly the existing fire laws, including regulations regarding the pollution of streams—a condition which exacerbated the inadequacy of the water supply—and automobiles parked in front of fire hydrants or near the fire engine houses. Chief Shipley further recommended that the Volunteer Firemen's Association encourage the Maryland General Assembly to pass legislation prohibiting "the sale of and setting off of fireworks in Howard County." By this time, Howard County was one of the few counties in the state that allowed fire-

1939 new location for the Howard County Volunteer Firemen's Association (8390 Main Street, circa 1944.

Association, the major event of 1939 was the completion of the new engine house at 210 Main Street (8390 Main Street). Designed by architect Herbert G. Jory and built by the Mancini Construction Company, the engine house—the third one since the formation of the Volunteer Fire Company No. 1 in 1888—cost approximately $43,000, and was completed in April 1939. It featured a kitchen in the basement, with meeting rooms and an office on the first floor. On the second floor, there was an apartment for Chief Shipley and his wife, and a dormitory and locker room for the men.

On April 25, the opening of the firehouse was celebrated with the Ladies' Auxiliary's annual banquet. Numerous prominent local business and political leaders were among the guests, including Reverend James W. Minter, chaplain of the Maryland State Firemen's Association. Following the dinner, the firemen and the Auxiliary presented Chief and Mrs. Shipley with a mirror for their apartment. Several speakers praised the work of the Firemen's Association in maintaining the security of Ellicott City and Howard County. From that time on, the Ladies' Auxiliary held their meetings at the engine house, instead of the courthouse. The firehouse was formally dedicated May 1, 1940 (after a full winter season to test the building's heating plant and plumbing). Nearly one hundred local residents attended the dedication ceremony, which featured a dinner served by the Ladies' Auxiliary, music provided by the Dickey Textile Band (from W. J. Dickey Woolen Mills in Oella), and speeches by government and Firemen's Association officials, including County Commissioner H. Grafton Penny, Paul J. Stromberg, T. Hunt Mayfield Jr., and J. Edwin Kroh.

There were few serious fires in Howard County during the spring and summer of 1939. Nevertheless, Chief Shipley continued his efforts to promote fire prevention whenever possible. In September, Chief Shipley was installed as president of the Fire Chief's Club of Maryland. Accordingly, the club announced that it was sponsoring an essay contest on fire prevention for high school students throughout the state. Shortly thereafter, the Howard County Fire Department announced that it was sponsoring a series of activities in conjunction with the annual observance of Fire Prevention Week. The firemen designed a display of fire hazards and

Above and Below: Sections of the original James H. Gaither's Express Office and Livery Stable (8267 Main Street) being demolished on the site of the new post office building, circa 1939.

fire prevention equipment in the windows of Hope's Hardware Store (8141 Main Street) and Samuel J. Yates' Store (8249 Main Street), and delivered a series of talks of fire prevention at the engine house itself.

But the most newsworthy event of the week was the lengthy interview of Chief Shipley in the *Ellicott City Times*. During the course of this interview, Shipley repeatedly pointed out the appalling danger posed by the town's inadequate

This cleared site for the new post office building has an irregular shape with a frontage of 106 feet on Main Street and 208 feet on Hamilton Street, circa 1939.

water system. As Chief Shipley explained, only good fortune and the skill of the local firefighters had prevented a disastrous fire in Ellicott City, which had not suffered a serious fire since 1924. While Chief Shipley promised that the Fire Department would remain as efficient in the future as it had ever been, he could not promise that the town's run of good luck would continue. "If a fire ever gets any serious headway in Ellicott City while the town still has its present water system," Shipley charged, "there

is no telling where it will stop. It's probable the entire town will be destroyed." In reviewing the town's water system, Shipley noted the complete lack of water facilities in several sections of Ellicott City, the insufficient supply of water at all of the town's fire hydrants, and the unreliability of the supply at all times. Moreover, the inadequate water supply made it impossible for other fire companies to render aid in case of a really extensive blaze. "As soon as we tap one hydrant," noted Chief Shipley, "no water can be had from any other in town. . . . The mains are so old and so small that the greatest volume we can get even at the lowest section is only about one-fourth the amount needed by a single engine company."

"This is not the worst of the situation, though," Chief Shipley continued. "On Columbia Pike, where there has been considerable building lately, there are no hydrants at all. Several other residential sections are not served by the present water system. That means the people living there actually have no fire protection." To solve the problem, Chief Shipley suggested that new mains be installed to connect Ellicott City with the Baltimore City water supply, a solution that eventually would be adopted. Chief Shipley admitted that the process would be costly, but he suggested that the additional fire protection would bring lower insurance rates, as well as other benefits that would more than recompense the county for the initial expense. "The least that the town could do would be hire an engineer to make a survey and estimate the cost of a new system," Shipley concluded. "It certainly can count on the full support of the Fire Department in any effort to improve the situation."

As if Chief Shipley had been a prophet, a major fire struck Ellicott City less than two weeks after his warning was published. On the afternoon of

Dedication of Ellicott City's Main U.S. Post Office, December 7, 1940. Luncheon was served at the firehouse (8390 Main Street) by the Ladies Auxiliary to the Ellicott City Volunteer Firemen's Association.

Saturday, October 14, 1939, St. Peter's Episcopal Church on St. Peter's Street (St. Paul Place)—a Tudor Gothic building, consecrated in 1854—was consumed by fire. The fire apparently began in the church furnace and spread when a spark from the chimney blew onto the shingle roof. Alerted to the danger, the rector of the church, Reverend Julius A. Velasco, summoned the Fire Department immediately. The volunteers made excellent time getting to the scene. As soon as they arrived, they connected a hose to the hydrant that was on a two-inch public water main about two hundred yards from the fire across from the intersection of College Avenue and Werner Street (Ross Road). "For about fifteen minutes we got a thin stream of water—about as much as you would get from an ordinary garden hose," Chief Shipley later recalled. "Then it ran out completely."

All the firefighters could do was watch the church building burn. "That was the worst part of it all, watching the church burn and knowing that we were helpless without water," mourned Reverend Velasco. "Of course we salvaged many things, as many as we could carry before it became too dangerous to enter the building, but in the end the building and its contents were a total loss." In a last-ditch effort to save the church, the firemen ran a hose from another hydrant on Main Street, nearly two thousand feet away, but by that time the fire had gained so much headway that they finally gave up. The church was subsequently rebuilt at the intersection of Rogers Avenue and Frederick Road. Bad luck dogged it there, too, however; in 1952, the church suffered another fire which caused extensive damage to its roof and upper floor.

The fire at St. Peter's Episcopal Church was the first serious fire in Ellicott City since 1933, but in the first four months of 1940, a series of major conflagrations struck the town. First, a fire broke out in the Times Building at 94 Main Street (8156 Main Street),

John LaVinka Home and Grocery Store fire (10107 Frederick Road) Pine Orchard.

The 1940 multiple alarm fire on Main Street and Columbia Pike.

where the *Ellicott City Times* was published. The flames subsequently spread to the post office and the offices of the Melville Scott & Son Insurance Agency. In battling the blaze, the firefighters were hampered by a careless motorist who had heedlessly parked in front of the nearest fire hydrant, in front of Caplan's (8125 Main Street). To connect the fire hose to the hydrant, a firefighter had to open the two front doors of the illegally parked vehicle, and run the hose through the automobile to the hydrant. Although the post office suffered extensive fire and smoke damage, no mail was destroyed. The *Times* Building was less fortunate, as the fire consumed much of the newspaper's archives. Only the prompt action of the volunteer firemen saved other

homes and businesses in the fire's path. "If it had not been for the thorough knowledge of combating such a destructive menace as fire, which training the young men of the department have obtained," testified Milton H. Easton, owner of one of Ellicott City's funeral homes, "the fire would not only have ruined my building, but all surrounding ones."

Less than two weeks later, the home of John LaVinka and his family caught fire on the afternoon of January 21. Located on Frederick Road, in Pine Orchard, the building also housed LaVinka's store—one of the oldest retail establishments in Howard County—which was located on the first floor. Chief Shipley and his men arrived in plenty of time to control the fire, but once again the lack of an adequate water supply hindered their efforts. The firefighters expended all the water in the tanks carried by the trucks, and even connected hoses that stretched all the way to the Little Patuxent River, nearly a mile away, but by the time they had finished, a high wind had swept the fire out of control.

On the evening of January 27, a fire broke out in a two-story frame dwelling owned by George W. Carr in the western section of Ellicott City (8400 Frederick Road). The flames spread so quickly that the occupants of the house had no time to get dressed, escaping into the freezing night temperatures in their night clothes. For a while the flames threatened Burgess' Garage (8444 Frederick Road), but again the firefighters managed to quell the blaze before it could spread.

The final fire in this disastrous 1940 sequence occurred April 5. Shortly before dawn, Mr. Der Wong—the Chinese laundryman whose establishment had been a landmark in the 100 block of Ellicott City (8225 Main Street) for decades—was awakened by the smell of smoke and the sound of crackling flames. Mr. Wong promptly alerted F. C. Higinbothom, who lived nearby above his funeral parlor. When he realized what was happening, Mr. Higinbothom immediately notified the Fire Department and then fled with his wife into the street.

Less fortunate were Joseph Berger and his wife, who owned the grocery store next door to Der Wong. Like the Higinbothoms, the Bergers had a residence on the second floor of their business, with John W. Hillsinger, a boarder, living there. By the time Mr. Hillsinger and the Bergers awoke, the flames and billowing smoke made it impossible for them to get downstairs. The firefighters' first task was to raise a ladder and rescue the frantic trio.

Meanwhile, the smoke had grown so thick that a substantial portion of Main Street was "blacked out." Blown by a strong east wind, the smoke filled several homes west of the Bergers residence, and the fire itself threatened the Church of God—located on the other side of Der Wong's laundry—and the Standard Oil service station, which stood at the corner of Columbia Pike. More than a dozen residents who lived in the line of the fire began evacuating their homes. Aided by fire companies from Catonsville, Jessup, and Savage, Chief Shipley attempted to bring as much water as possible to play upon the flames, directing his men to pump water from the Patapsco River, the Tiber Branch, and the Cat Rocks Stream as well as the nearby hydrants on Main Street. One of the top priorities was to keep the flames from reaching the fuel tanks of the Standard Oil gas station.

By 8:30 A.M. the combined efforts of the fire companies had brought the fire under control, but the volunteer firemen stayed on the scene to extinguish the occasional flare-ups that occurred within the embers. In the end, the Bergers' grocery and Der Wong's laundry were almost totally destroyed, and the roof of the Church of God suffered severe damage.

For the rest of the year, there were no major fires in or around Ellicott City, but the training and modernization of the Fire Department continued apace. At the end of May 1940, fifteen members of the Ellicott City volunteer company received certificates attesting to their completion of the University of Maryland training course. Simultaneously, the firefighters began another training procedure, to familiarize themselves with a used ladder truck they were planning to purchase from the Hagerstown Fire Department. Up to that point, the county only possessed light ladders, which could reach a maximum height of twenty-four feet.

The truck—an American LaFrance "Type 14" City Service ladder truck—was able to hold about a dozen heavy ladders, the longest of which could reach 55 feet; together, the ladders totaled 265 ground feet. The truck also

Looking east from the Patapsco River Bridge at Route 40 under construction. Single lane road from Rolling Road to Rogers Avenue was completed in November 1938, circa 1938.

could carry 500 feet of hose. To further enhance its effectiveness, the Association elected to add a turret pipe with a revolving nozzle that could deliver a stream of five hundred gallons of water per minute with as much as three hundred pounds of pressure, thereby enabling Howard County firefighters to direct a controlled stream of water upon virtually any fire from a safe distance. After purchasing the ladder truck for only five hundred dollars, the Association placed it into service on November 20, 1940.

Meanwhile, the Ellicott City Fire Department continued to have trouble obtaining sufficient volunteers to answer fire alarms during the working day. By the summer of 1940, the American economy had begun to revive under the stimulus of increased defense production, spurred by the Roosevelt administration's strategic preparedness program. Employment statistics rose sharply, and numerous employees began working overtime to keep up with the rising demand for both military hardware and consumer goods. With more local residents employed outside the area, and with employees reluctant to lose their workers for any significant period of time during the workday, the Fire Department began searching for alternative means of obtaining volunteer firefighters.

One measure which seemed to promise relief was the formation in July 1940 of a reserve unit of firemen under the direction of Chief Shipley. This group, which consisted of Ellicott City businessmen and their employees, offered to answer all alarms that came in from 7:00 A.M. to 6:00 P.M. from an area bounded by the Patapsco River on one end, to Rogers Avenue on the other. After they had completed their training, Chief Shipley promised to make the reserves full members of the Fire Department.

In late 1940, Congress voted to extend the life of the Selective Service Act, thereby bringing an increasing number of young American men into the nation's armed services. Others, including numerous members of the Howard County Volunteer Firemen's Association, were assigned to jobs in defense plants in and around Baltimore City, such as the Martin Marietta Corporation or Bethlehem Steel. As the ranks of volunteer firemen dwindled, Chief Shipley sought ways to further reduce the demands on the Fire Department's strained resources. In February 1941, he issued a public statement urging county residents to be extremely cautious in starting brush fires. "It is about all the boys can do to get a single engine out, fully manned, for an ordinary call," reported the *Ellicott City Times*. And if that one engine was forced to respond to a relatively unimportant brush fire, the rest of the county lacked any viable protection. "Give the boys a break by not starting any fire that you cannot control yourselves," continued the *Times*. "And don't start any fires at all when the wind is strong." Despite Shipley's advice, an epidemic of brush fires swept Howard County in the late winter and early spring of 1941, as residents sought to clean up their fields with little heed to the potential consequences of their thoughtless actions. The one optimistic note came from the fact that most of the brush fires were started on weekends or after normal working hours, when more of the regular firefighters were available for duty.

The only serious fire that occurred in the early spring of 1941 was a house fire that destroyed a single family home (3943 College Avenue). Once again, the firefighters were hindered by the meager supply of water from the town's public water system. But at the end of May, disaster struck as Ellicott City suffered one of the worst fires in the history of the town.

Across the Patapsco River, on Frederick Road just inside the Baltimore County line, stood an eight-story plant and machine shop owned by the Doughnut Corporation of America. The plant employed nearly 450 men, many of them residents of Ellicott City, and the machine shop had recently begun to produce defense material for the U.S. Army. On Tuesday afternoon, May 27, a fire began in a pile of lumber adjoining the machine shop. DCA employees spotted the blaze about 3:30 P.M., and initially attempted to fight the fire themselves. But the flames quickly spread to the B & O Railroad siding next to the lumber pile; within seconds the fire had ignited eleven freight cars—loaded with doughnut and cake mix—on the siding.

The fire then advanced to the machine shop, leaving it nothing but a twisted mass of molten machinery and sagging steel girders. Five automobiles parked in the rear of the main building also were consumed. Next came the main building itself. By this time the Ellicott City firefighters had arrived on the scene. Realizing that the main danger lay in the ignition of the eight concrete grain elevators, which together contained approximately 300,000 bushels of wheat that could produce a disastrous explosion, the volunteer firemen worked frantically to keep the flames away from the elevators.

Once again their efforts were ham-

Doughnut Corporation of America (Wilkens Rodgers) 27 Frederick Road after a May 1941 fire caused estimated damage of $3.5 million.

pered by the absence of a reliable water supply; when the firemen tried to obtain water from the hydrants nearby, they got nothing but a meager trickle. Instead, they quickly lay a line of hose to the Patapsco River and began pumping water from the river. Within an hour, fire companies from Catonsville, Arbutus, Sykesville, Savage, Pikesville, Cockeysville, Violetville, Woodstock, and Baltimore City had responded to the alarm, dispatching a total of thirty fire trucks.

By that time the fire had reached the cereal plant in the main building and the flour mill, sending the flames roaring throughout the structure. On the seventh floor, the flames ignited several hundred drums of shortening—each containing 450 pounds of the highly flammable substance. As night fell, residents could see the flames and smoke billowing from the plant for miles around. For those in Ellicott City, the flames were virtually the only light they had. In an attempt to prevent short circuits in the town's electrical system, authorities had cut power to businesses and homes.

Those who witnessed the conflagration never forgot it. Chief Fritz Maisel of the Baltimore County Fire Department later testified that the DCA fire was the largest blaze he had ever fought,

and the only one he could not control. The firefighters did manage to save the eight grain elevators, but the machine shop was completely destroyed, and would never be rebuilt. Three volunteer firemen had to receive medical treatment after being overcome by gas fumes, and two DCA employees were treated for minor injuries. DCA officials promised to reopen the plant as soon as they could make repairs, and they retained most of their employees on the DCA payroll, using them to help clear away the charred debris and install new equipment. The total financial loss to the company was finally reckoned at $3.5 million.

The 1941 American LaFrance pumper that is now on display at the Fire Museum of Maryland, Lutherville, Maryland.

SIX
1941-1960

By the autumn of 1941, the clouds of war had begun to descend over the United States. As the Roosevelt administration increased its aid to Great Britain, relations with Nazi Germany continued to deteriorate. In the Far East, the American refusal to countenance Japanese ambitions in China and Southeast Asia led the government in Tokyo to commence planning for a surprise attack on American naval forces stationed at Pearl Harbor. Throughout the United States, the watchword was preparedness. Draft calls increased, the National and State Guards stepped up their recruitment efforts, and special civil defense units were formed, including airplane observers and post watchers.

In accordance with the renewed emphasis on preparedness, the Howard County Volunteer Firemen's Association established an Auxiliary Fire Service Unit. Officials hoped to recruit 175 men to staff the Auxiliary Unit. All male county residents who were not eligible for the draft—and who had not enrolled in any other civil defense organization—were urged to enlist in the new firefighting brigade. Members of the Auxiliary Fire Service Unit were expected to devote one hour a week, for five weeks, to basic training by Chief Shipley, including the handling of ladders and hose, and instructions on the best way to extinguish incendiary bombs in the event of an airborne enemy attack. Again, Chief Shipley pleaded with county residents to exercise extreme caution in starting any brush fires that might require assistance from the volunteer firemen, who remained short-staffed due to the manpower crunch.

To assist their regular and auxiliary firefighters, the Howard County

The 1941 multiple alarm fire—lower Main Street (8059–8069 Main Street).

The blaze broke out in the back of Roy's Cafe, a tavern and poolroom owned by Roy Radcliff on the south side of Main Street, near Maryland Avenue. From there it spread to the Earle Theater—Ellicott City's oldest theater, formerly owned by Edwin A. Rodey—which had recently been refurbished by its new owner, Jackson D. Wheat. The flames then advanced to the Easton Son's Funeral Home, causing severe damage to the lovely chapel that had witnessed so many of the town's funeral services in recent decades. The fire also damaged the second and third floors of the build-

Volunteer Firemen's Association sold one of its older, less efficient fire trucks, and purchased another new fire engine. This American LaFrance engine, which arrived in mid-November 1941, was equipped with a 12-cylinder, 202-horsepower motor. It also featured a 500-gallon per minute pump, a 100-gallon booster tank, and a 1,500-foot capacity hose body. (This engine is on display at the Fire Museum of Maryland, 1301 York Road, Lutherville, Maryland.) Prior to the delivery of the 1941 engine, the federal government considered using it due to the impending war emergency. The Howard County Volunteer Firemen's Association outlined the needs for this equipment, however, and the government permitted it to be delivered to Ellicott City.

The Fire Department needed all the help it could get in the early morning hours of December 30, 1941. A devastating fire broke out in the lower (east) end of Ellicott City's business district.

The 1941 multiple alarm fire—lower Main Street (8059–8069 Main Street). View from Tiber Alley.

ing, which served as the residence of Mr. and Mrs. Clinton M. Easton.

As soon as Chief Shipley noted the extent of the fire, he telephoned to the Catonsville, Jessup, and Savage companies for assistance. The Ellicott City firefighters laid a hose to the Patapsco River, and began pumping water onto the blaze. It was so cold, however, that the water froze in a sheet as soon as it hit the street and formed icicles on the telephone and trolley wires. At one point, the telephone cables collapsed, cutting off service to much of Ellicott City. To avoid further confusion and injury, police closed the Patapsco River bridge and rerouted automobile traffic over the Edmondson Avenue (Route 40) extension.

While the combined forces of the fire companies battled the blaze, apprehensive residents of adjoining buildings fled into the street. Smoke drove out the Coroneos family, who operated a restaurant below their apartment, as well as Walter S. Fissel and his family, and several elderly women who lived in the home of Mrs. Bessie Willis. Fortunately, Mr. Clinton M. Easton and his wife were not home that evening; both were on air-raid duty at a nearby observation post when the fire broke out, and Mrs. Easton remained at her post while her husband hurried to the scene of the

View of "Tongue Row," Columbia Pike, snowstorm Palm Sunday, March 30, 1942.

View of "Missionary Bottom," Merryman Street, snowstorm Palm Sunday, March 30, 1942 .

fire. After three hours, the firefighters finally brought the fire under control, but the theater and tavern were completely ruined.

By this time the nation was at war. On December 7, 1941, a squadron of Japanese bombers had attacked the American naval base at Pearl Harbor; the following day, President Roosevelt asked Congress for a declaration of war against Japan. Several days later, the government of Nazi Germany, bound by an alliance to Japan, responded by declaring war against the United States. For several months, Americans on the East Coast feared an attack by Germany, either by plane or U-boat, and officials redoubled their civil defense precautions accordingly.

Unfortunately for the Fire Department, Howard Countians chose this moment to call in a record number of fire alarms. For the first three months of 1942 alone, the Howard County Volunteer Firemen's Association tallied 178 calls. In a county with a total population of 18,000 people, this represented an appalling misuse of the firefighters' time and energy. Obviously the Ellicott City Company alone could not handle all these calls. Chief Shipley found it necessary to frequently call in assistance from the Savage, Halethorpe, Jessup and Laurel companies. To make matters worse, nearly 20 percent of these fires started in chimneys and, as Chief Shipley pointed out, all of them "could have been avoided with just a little care on the part of the occupants who should have the chimney cleaned at least twice each year. . . . It is imperative that we prevent fires now," Shipley concluded sternly, "and that as much help as possible be given in extinguishing fires that do start, particularly in view of the shortage of volunteer firemen."

Apparently Howard County residents heeded Chief Shipley's advice, because there were no major fires in the county for the duration of the war. The war years did, however, witness the establishment of additional fire companies in Elkridge (1942), West Friendship (1944), and Lisbon (1944).

Initially, several of the companies found it necessary to start operations in less than ideal surroundings. When the Lisbon Company was formed, its fire truck was a civil defense engine assigned to the county, which was housed in the garage of one of its members. By the time the war ended, however, each Company possessed a siren with the capability of carrying sound for a considerable distance. With controls either at the firehouse or a remote location, the time between receipt of a call and the sounding of an alarm was reduced significantly. Several of the alarms were designed so that the telephone call that alerted firemen to the danger also activated the alarm signal. The Ellicott City Company also possessed two-way radio equipment which had been constructed and installed on its apparatus by William Bazzell, an amateur radio operator who held a license from the Federal Radio Commission.

The establishment of these fire companies also led to the reorganization of the Howard County Volunteer Firemen's Association. Since there were now five separate companies, the original Ellicott City Company decided to reestablish itself as a separate entity. Hence, on October 21, 1943, the Board of Directors of the Howard County Volunteer Firemen's Association voted to amend its charter by striking out the words "Howard County" and inserting the words "Ellicott City"; its name henceforth would be "the Ellicott City Volunteer Firemen's Association, Inc." At its annual meeting January 5, 1944, the members of the Association ratified the change.

In the spring of 1944, the companies then joined together to form the Howard County Volunteer Firemen's Association. Chief B. H. Shipley was

Howard House (8202 Main Street), showing second floor porch with iron railing that was removed during World War II.

named temporary president until the Association could hold its first annual convention in September. At that convention, the Association elected Dr. E. A. Nitsch, a pharmacist from Elkridge, president of the Association.

The war years also saw changes in the operations of the Ladies' Auxiliary. During the war, the Volunteer Firemen's Association discontinued its annual car-

Western Terminus operator switching overhead trolley pole to electric line. Note the sand storage box (8390 Main Street).

nivals, due to a shortage of personnel. To help alleviate the resulting shortfall in funds for the Association, the Auxiliary sponsored a three-day "Street Fair" in 1943, which brought in a profit of approximately $3,000. It subsequent-

ly sponsored similar fairs in 1944 and 1945, each time earning a profit of at least $2,700. All the funds were turned over to the fire company to use as it saw fit. Furthermore, the Auxiliary made special contributions to the United Servicemen's Organization and the American Red Cross during the war. And as the firefighters themselves reorganized on a county wide basis, so did the women. They formed their own Ladies' Auxiliary to the Howard County Volunteer Firemen's Association October 3, 1944. On the state level, two members of the Auxiliary were elected to serve as president of the Ladies' Auxiliary to the Maryland State Firemen's Association: Mrs. Mildred A. Brust (1939–1940) and Mrs. Mae R. Schoene (1946–1947).

In May 1945, the war in Europe ended with the unconditional surrender

Western Terminus waiting station and No. 9 Trolley (8390 Main Street). For years, every Saturday evening, rain or shine, local resident Ola Cole left her home in "Missionary Bottom," Merryman Street, and sat in the waiting station to greet her many friends passing by. Photo circa 1946.

No. 9 Trolley on trestle bridge approaching Oella Avenue, circa 1950.

On December 6, 1945, the first major fire in Howard County in nearly four years broke out in the buildings of the Howard County Farmer's Cooperative, located on the northeast corner of Frederick Road and St. John's Lane (at the present site of the Southern States Cooperative—9064 Frederick Road). The fire began shortly after sunset, and soon the flames were rushing through two barns—one of which contained a substantial quantity of seed corn and baled hay—and a pair of smaller buildings, including a drying plant. Although the Ellicott City Fire Company responded quickly, they found

of Germany. Three months later, the Japanese government also surrendered following the use of two atomic bombs against the cities of Hiroshima and Nagasaki. Although the end of the war touched off a wave of unrestrained celebrations across the nation, the adjustment to a peacetime economy proved far more difficult than many expected. By the end of 1945, the United States was experiencing a bewildering combination of inflation, consumer shortages, and rising unemployment. And as servicemen returned home in increasing numbers, they found that the traditional American family roles had changed; women who had worked in defense plants during the war had developed a taste for independence, and their children knew far more about world events than most adults had known before 1941.

Trolley tracks alongside Westchester Avenue, circa 1956.

themselves again short of water. Unfortunately, the usual source of water in that area, MacCubbin's Ice Pond (3602–3606 St. John's Lane), had been drained several days earlier. Given the lack of water and the volatile nature of the stored grain, there was little the firefighters could do, despite the heavy downpour that soaked the men as the four buildings burned to the ground.

Another fire erupted in the downtown area of Ellicott City eight days later. On the morning of December 14, an overheated oil stove sent flames swirling through the Pentecostal Church at 309 Main Street (8515 Frederick Road). The church's pastor, the Reverend James T. Wilson, lived above the church with his wife. Before the Ellicott City firefighters could extinguish the blaze, it had destroyed the entire three-story structure. Nevertheless, the Fire Company—aided by their Baltimore County brethren— did manage to save the frame building next door from the flames.

There would be no more major fires in Howard County for another eight years. At the start of this prolonged period of good fortune, the Ellicott City Volunteer Firemen's Association was led by William F. Kirkwood (president), Charles E. Miller (vice president), William F. Kirkwood Jr. (secretary), and

former chief Dr. Benjamin Mellor Jr., who served as treasurer. Chief B. H. Shipley still supervised the operations of the Fire Department, aided by his son, who served as captain, and Lieutenants T. W. Collette and William F. Collette. The active department's engineers included Charles P. Ditch, William C. Holmes, Charles A. Klein, and Henry L. Miller.

As an indication of the reputation for fire prevention, which Chief Shipley had acquired during his tenure with the Fire Company, President Harry S Truman (who had succeeded the late Franklin D. Roosevelt in April 1945) invited Shipley to attend the sessions of the National Conference on Fire Prevention, which the federal government sponsored in May 1947. Under Chief Shipley's guidance, the other members of the Ellicott City Volunteer Firemen's Association continued to improve their own knowledge of firefighting techniques. Nine more members of the Company received merit award cards for completing the University of Maryland's fire service course in June.

Later in the summer of 1947, the Fifth District—which had unsuccessfully attempted to form a fire company in the spring of 1928—finally organized its own volunteer fire department, based in

Clarksville. The establishment of this company gave the county a firefighting organization in every district. For its part, the Ellicott City Fire Department upgraded its own equipment by purchasing in December 1947 another new fire engine. With a 500-gallon booster tank, a 500-gallon three-stage centrifugal pump, one thousand feet of hose, a special chassis and a 225-horsepower motor, the new engine carried the most comprehensive line of firefighting equipment ever used in Howard County. According to Chief Shipley, it was intended to provide the Department with a more effective means of fighting fires in the recently constructed homes on the hilly sections on the outskirts of Ellicott City, where water was still in abysmally short supply.

It could have been the last piece of new equipment the Fire Company purchased for quite some time. In the summer of 1948, a dispute emerged over the use of games of chance by volunteer or fraternal organizations, including the Ellicott City Volunteer Firemen's Association, which had long used such games at its annual carnival. There was, in short, a legal question as to whether a sponsoring organization could profit from these events. The issue was submitted to the voters in a referendum in November 1948, and in preparation for

that vote, the fire departments from Ellicott City, Lisbon, and West Friendship joined in an appeal to the public to support the fire departments' position. Reminding voters that 75 percent of the fire departments' funding came from their annual carnivals (with another $1,000–1,500 coming from county funds, distributed by the County Commissioners), the fire companies warned that the discontinuance of the carnivals inevitably would result in higher taxation. To protect themselves until the issue was resolved, the fire companies also canceled their carnivals for 1948.

In the meantime, the Ellicott City Volunteer Firemen enjoyed a rare respite from the sound of the alarm. From May 28 to September 30, there were no fire emergencies at all in or around the town. Indeed, the only fire that occurred during the autumn of 1948 was a chimney fire that was quickly extinguished without serious damage. For the entire year, the Ellicott City Fire Department received only sixty-three alarms, forty-eight of which came from the Second District, including eight dwelling fires, fifteen chimney fires, thirteen field fires, four automobile fires, five fires from oil stoves and one from an overheated electric motor.

As the Ellicott City Volunteer Fire

Department entered its twenty-fifth year, Chief Shipley paused to reflect in his annual report upon the accomplishments of the organization. Unlike many organizations which diminished or deteriorated with age, the Fire Company's responsibilities—particularly in the fields of fire prevention and education—had grown since its reorganization in 1924. "From a small beginning," he wrote, "we have developed in the last decade an influence and helpfulness that radiates and circulates technical information to all in our community in regards [to] fire protection and fire prevention, and many continuously seek our advice." While local industrial concerns had gone far toward solving most of their fire protection problems, Chief Shipley noted with regret that Ellicott City's numerous commercial enterprises—with their tradition of "rugged individualism"—still found it difficult to cooperate in the area of fire prevention. And even though the general public in and around Ellicott City had adopted a more enlightened attitude toward fire protection in recent years, there remained several public safety issues that needed to be addressed by the Volunteer Firemen's Association and the county government.

First, Chief Shipley pointed out, the distribution of the region's water supply remained inadequate. "You will find many sections of your community with no water supply whatever," noted Chief Shipley. Moreover, "you will find that in your mercantile district that the size and capacity of the present water mains could very easily lead to a conflagration." In other words, the six-inch mains that the town had installed were far less efficient, carrying less than half as much water than the eight-inch mains that were available for only a slight increase in cost. Until the existing mains could be replaced, Chief Shipley recommended that they be thoroughly cleaned out, since accumulated deposits already had cut their carrying capacity between 40 and 60 percent.

Chief Shipley also recommended that outlying sections of Ellicott City that lacked any water distribution system whatsoever should be supplied with concrete cisterns of thirty-thousand-gallon capacity for the use of firefighters. To ensure that firemen could reach the cisterns in all kinds of weather, Chief Shipley asked that they be constructed on hard surface roads. To further reduce the potential of fires, Chief Shipley suggested that all dilapidated buildings be torn down and all "blighted areas" be eliminated. Finally, Chief Shipley asked each community to establish a committee "consisting of the heads of the Health, Police, Building, Engineering, and Fire Departments to pass judgement upon all buildings, premises or business, where a license is required, and all matters that affect the health, safety and general well-being of the community."

Even though Chief Shipley insisted that much more work remained to be done in the area of fire prevention, his efforts—and those of his colleagues—continued to pay dividends. Once again an entire year passed with no serious fires in Ellicott City.

On September 14, 1949, the Ellicott City Volunteer Firemen's Association celebrated its twenty-fifth anniversary at a dinner meeting at Hardman's Restaurant, at Baltimore National Pike and St. John's Lane (9150 Baltimore National Pike). Former chief Benjamin Mellor Jr. served as toastmaster, and the principal speaker was Dr. Harry C. Byrd, president of the University of Maryland. One of the highlights of the evening was the presentation of a lovely silver platter to Chief Shipley and his wife, Mary, in honor of their service to the community. The Association also had reason to celebrate the purchase of yet another new engine, an Oren/Available "Model 1600" triple combination pumper, with the capability of pumping 750 gallons of water per minute.

The total cost of the new engine was $13,549, most of which came from the proceeds of the Association's annual carnival, supplemented by funds raised by the Ladies' Auxiliary. The Association had resumed its carnival in 1949, following the resolution of the legal problems that had forced its cancellation the previous year, but the Association now decided to obtain its own permanent site for the carnival. Accordingly, the Board of Directors of the Ellicott City Volunteer Firemen's Association voted October 26, 1950, to purchase twenty-two and one-half acres of land on Montgomery Road, adjoining the grounds of the Ellicott City Junior High School (Ellicott Mills Middle School, 4445 Montgomery Road).

The lot—which was nearly level and provided adequate facilities for both parking and carnival activities—had been owned by Dr. Benjamin Mellor Jr., Charles E. Miller, and their wives, who agreed to sell it to the Association for approximately $4,000. (At that time, Mr. Miller served both as president of the Association's Board of Directors and a member of the Board of Commissioners for Howard County. To avoid any appearance of a conflict of interest—from serving on the board of an organization that received funds from the county government—the Association agreed to waive their annual allotment from the county for the time being. The Association's annual carnival was held on the new site in the summer of 1950, and proved immensely successful, setting new attendance records, and netting nearly $8,000 in profits for the organization.

During 1950, the Ellicott City Volunteer Firemen's Association also voted to solve a space problem for the county government. Due to a rise in the number of crimes committed by teenagers in Howard County, local officials were contemplating the establishment of a juvenile detention center in the courthouse. The only place they could hold the juveniles, however, was the former judge's offices, which had long been used as sleeping quarters for jurors who had to remain at the courthouse overnight. The Fire Department offered to provide sleeping accommodations for the jurors at its engine house, but Chief Shipley adamantly refused to accept the beds stored at the courthouse "because of the unsanitary condition of the beds in question." Accordingly, the County Commissioners agreed to purchase new beds for the jurors, and the deal was completed.

In 1951, the county's fire companies took an additional step toward coordination of their services with the establishment of a two-way radio communication system. The system also served as part of the county's civil defense program. This move was indeed timely, for the whole issue of civil defense had received renewed attention throughout the United States following the Soviet Union's explosion of a nuclear test device in the summer of 1949. Once the two-way radio system went into effect, the county's Fire Department could serve as a communications center in the event of an emergency. At the end of 1951, the Fire Department also purchased a new, smaller engine, a 250-gallon per minute Triple Combination Oren/Chevrolet "mini" pumper, for a cost of $8,147.

The following year was a relatively quiet one for the men of the Ellicott City Volunteer Firemen's Association. They answered fifty-nine alarms in 1952, but less than $10,000 in property was lost. More than one-fourth of the fires were field fires, with dwelling/house fires and auto fires close behind.

Unfortunately, 1952 also saw the tragic deaths of five children in a terrifying house fire on Sunday, April 20. Shortly before noon, an oil stove exploded in a one-room log cabin home on New Cut Road. Both of the parents were out of the house at the time, but four of their children, aged two months to three years, were in the cabin at the time the fire began. Although the par-

Removing mud and debris from the bridge over the Patapsco River after the September 1, 1952, flood. Large building, rear, is the Continental Milling Company processing "Polka-Dot" Feeds.

Carolinas early in the holiday weekend. As the storm intensified, a drenching rain struck Ellicott City on Sunday. That evening, the downpour increased in fury, culminating in a cloudburst early Monday morning. Lower Main Street began to flood shortly before dawn. By 5:00 A.M. the water had backed all the way up to the Patapsco National Bank (8098 Main Street). It then crashed through the windows of Valmas Brothers Lunch, Rosentock's, David's Jewelry, and the Howard County Library (8089–8109 Main Street), sweeping merchandise—including rings and necklaces—out into the street.

As the rain continued, the garage in back of Kraft's Meat Store (8081 Main Street) slid into the Tiber Branch, blocking the stream and causing a further backup on Main Street. By 5:30,

ents rushed back to their home as soon as they heard the explosion, the flames—leaping twenty feet into the air—prevented the father from entering the house. While he searched for a break in the inferno, another child, two years old, ran too close to the flames and she, too, was badly burned and later died at St. Agnes' Hospital in Baltimore City. By the time the firefighters arrived, the cabin already had burned nearly to the ground. The bodies of all four children were later recovered in the ruins.

The tragedy on New Cut Road was the only major fire of 1952, although members of the Ellicott City Fire Department spent nearly as much time fighting the flash flood that struck the town on Labor Day as they did battling fires the entire year. The flood resulted from a hurricane that smashed into the

Onlookers after the September 1, 1952, flood. At the right are the remains of the original center pier for the wooden covered bridge destroyed by fire in 1914.

when the Ellicott City Fire Department sounded its alarm, nearly two dozen automobiles that had been parked on the lower end of Main Street had been swept up and deposited in a massive pile under the Baltimore & Ohio Railroad bridge. When the firemen arrived, they began pumping water out of flooded basements. Aided by their colleagues from the Clarksville, West Friendship, and Elkridge stations, the firefighters used their hose lines to wash all the soil and debris from Main Street. The fire service also provided security until a unit of the Maryland National Guard arrived on the scene around noon.

On a more cheerful note, Captain B. H. Shipley Jr. was elected president of the Maryland State Firemen's Association at the organization's annual convention in Ocean City in June 1952. This was indeed a historic occasion, because the election of Captain Shipley marked the first and only time that the son of a former president of the State Association had been elected to the same office.

During his term as president, Captain Shipley made ninety-three official trips across the state, covering more than seven thousand miles; even then he had to decline invitations because of previous commitments. Like his father, Captain Shipley urged his colleagues to continue to press the cause of professional training of firefighters. "Some may be thinking firemenship is a 'snap'—that they have had all the training needed and that no further requirements are necessary," wrote Captain Shipley in his annual report. "The field is becoming more competitive and the more competitive it is—[the] higher the standards to be met." Specifically, Captain Shipley urged his associates to take advantage of the specialized training available through the Firemen's Training Committee, the successor organization to the Fire Service Extension Committee at the University of Maryland.

Captain Shipley also recommended that fire companies adopt a new strategy to promote the cause of fire protection—public relations, to increase communication and cooperation between firefighters and the general public. "The average citizen is becoming keenly conscious of the advantages today of having trained personnel in your local organizations," he noted. "Who has made John Q. Public conscious? It is the men of vision in the fire service who have not sat back and let things drift, but who have brought to the membership of the

Ellicott City Active Volunteer Firemen, left to right: Howard J. Massey Jr., Thomas E. Mullinix, George M. Cullum, and Elmer M. Cullum Jr. Note the canister type gas mask, circa 1952.

various fire departments facts to make them aware of the importance of their duties." To further enhance public awareness of fire protection activities, Captain Shipley suggested that "we should strive for approval of our activities by the public in the various towns and communities in our state. It is also of great importance that we stimulate a far larger percentage of our own membership to active participation in committee and Association work."

As strongly as Captain Shipley might urge fire companies to adopt modern and professional methods, the Ellicott City Fire Department still was plagued by several long-standing problems that seemed to defy solution. Just as the Fire Company had suffered from a lack of manpower during regular business hours in the 1930s and 1940s, so it now experienced difficulty securing sufficient men to answer fire alarms during weekdays. Once again the problem lay in the reluctance of local businessmen to allow their employees to leave their jobs to respond to fire emergencies. Sometimes, according to one official of the Volunteer Firemen's Association, the fire engines had to leave the station house with only two men on them. To encourage merchants to let the volunteer firefighters respond to alarms, the Association agreed to reimburse the employers for the time lost by their men

during emergencies.

And the perennial problem of inadequate water again arose when a fire broke out at the Howard County Freezer Locker Building at the corner of Frederick Road and St. John's Lane (9064 Frederick Road) on the morning of June 2, 1953. The blaze broke out in the attic of the building and quickly threatened the occupants of half a dozen apartments over the locker. By drafting water from a pond on St. John's Lane—formerly known as MacCubbin's Ice Pond (3602–3606 St. John's Lane)—the firefighters were able to use a fog nozzle to send a heavy spray of fog toward the burning building, thereby blowing away the thick black smoke that had hidden the flames from the firemen. But the water from the pond proved inadequate, and the firefighters had to adopt a shuttle system of sending one engine at a time to the hydrant opposite the Ellicott City Police Station (8316 Main Street) to refill their water tanks after they had been emptied into the blaze. After the fire was extinguished, Chief Shipley informed the County Commissioners that they should make sure the pond was always maintained in readiness for future fires in the area.

Then, on Christmas Eve, 1953, tragedy struck. In the late evening, two Howard County policemen on routine

Disastrous blaze—the remains of an eighteen-room house and contents (4020 Old Columbia Pike).

patrol noticed that the eighteen-room home of William F. Jacob and his family on Columbia Pike (4020 Old Columbia Pike) was on fire. While one of the policeman radioed to the Waterloo State Police Barracks for firefighting assistance, the other man ran into the house to inform Jacob and his wife of the danger.

Soon after the Ellicott City firemen arrived at the scene, Chief Shipley felt they had brought the flames under control. But suddenly the water tanks on the first fire engine gave out, and the fire regained its momentum. There were no other sources of water near the blaze,

and for the next few hours the firefighters shuttled water between a hydrant located in front of the Miller Chevrolet Sales (8307 Main Street) and the fire. Recognizing the danger, Chief Shipley radioed for help from other companies, notifying particularly those companies whose engines carried large water tanks. In all, thirteen engines responded to the alarm.

All to no avail. By 3:45 A.M. the fire had burned itself out and the house had been reduced to a mere shell. About an hour and a half earlier, Lieutenant

Joseph A. Stigler had been relieved from duty. Lt. Stigler returned to his home, changed into dry clothes and—being a dedicated volunteer officer—returned to the fire scene. By the time Lt. Stigler had returned, Captain Shipley and several other firemen were in back of the house, rolling up the fire hose, while four fire-fighters stood in front of the house, waiting for the fire engine to take them back to the station. "All of a sudden," Captain Shipley said, "I heard a heavy thud. I looked around and saw that one of the chimneys had fallen."

They rushed to the front and found all four firemen buried under a pile of bricks. One of the men, Charles P. Ditch, engineer, had been knocked unconscious; the other three were trying to extricate themselves. Ambulances were summoned immediately, and all four men were taken to St. Agnes Hospital. Two of the firemen—Mr. Ditch, who was forty-four years old, and Lt. Stigler, thirty-four—died from their injuries. Although the other two fire-fighters—Charles E. Ash and Charles A. Massey—survived, they suffered seri-ous injuries. Mr. Ash, especially, was in critical condition for more than a week, with a broken leg and ankle, head lacer-

Charles P. Ditch
1909–1953

ations, and internal injuries that required numerous blood transfusions. Mr. Massey suffered a broken leg and head lacerations.

It was the first and only time fire-fighters had been killed on the job since the Ellicott City Volunteer Firemen's Association had been founded. Mr. Ditch was the son of Mr. and Mrs. Purnell Ditch, and the husband of Dorothy M. (nee Miller) Ditch. He had one daughter, Beverly Ann Ditch. Lt. Stigler was the son of Teresa A. (nee Mooney) and the late Joseph E. Stigler. He and his wife, Mary Ann "Nancy" (nee McDermott) Stigler, had three children, Mary Beth Stigler, Jo Anne Stigler, and Joseph P. Stigler, who was born a few days after the accident.

Numerous local civic, fraternal, and service organizations offered to assist the bereaved families of the unfortunate men. Dr. Benjamin Mellor Jr., of the Ellicott City Volunteer Firemen's Association, coordinated the collection of contributions, and the Association itself paid the funeral and hospital expenses of their fallen colleagues. And the *Ellicott City Times* took the occasion to remind its readers of the sacrifices and risks that the volunteer firemen made for the community every time the fire alarm rang. "The truth for you is in the true meaning of volunteer fire service," explained the *Times*. "Stripped of all glamour, screaming sirens and flashing red lights, it means that being a volunteer fireman also means you may be required to lay down your life or that your life may be snatched from you by a

Joseph A. Stigler
1919–1953

rain of bricks from a chimney weakened by the collapse of a house. With all modern trappings which science has applied to firefighting, it still takes men with raw language—guts, to come to grips with the blaze and extinguish it. And it takes . . . a special kind of enthusiasm to be a volunteer fireman. . . The men who fell victim to a staggering pile of bricks on Christmas morning were of that breed. They and all like them, are a special kind of citizenry who put their lives on the line whenever the fire siren sounds."

On January 6, 1954, the Board of Directors of the Ellicott City Volunteer Firemen's Association appointed a special committee—consisting of Lloyd G. Taylor, B. H. Shipley, Dr. Benjamin Mellor Jr., and E. Reid Bossom—to secure a proper memorial commemorating the memories of Mr. Ditch and Lt. Stigler. Several months later, Mr. Taylor reported that he had obtained specifications from the International Bronze Tablet Company on a memorial plaque for the fallen firefighters. On July 1, Chief Shipley informed the Board of Directors that the bronze memorial plaque had been delivered. It was subsequently affixed to the firehouse in a special spot of honor.

The Ellicott City Volunteer Firemen's Association also established a special memorial trophy in the names of Lt. Ditch and Lt. Stigler, to be presented by the Association annually to the individual Howard County fireman who had "performed his duties in an outstanding manner, bringing credit to the fire service of Howard County or the state of Maryland." There were also two additional trophies awarded by the Howard County Volunteer Firemen's Association: the B. H. Shipley Trophy, awarded annually by the County Association "for the most heroic and outstanding act performed beyond the ordinary duty of a fireman," and the Savage Trophy, for "the outstanding fireman in Howard County."

As a practical matter, however, the Ellicott City Volunteer Firemen's Association still was having trouble obtaining volunteers for fire emergencies during weekdays. Again, the problem centered on the unwillingness of employers to lose their workers during the daytime. The shortage was especially acute for qualified drivers for the fire engines. The problem reached crisis proportions in early 1954, because of the sudden increase in fire alarms. It was, in fact, a particularly busy year for fires, as the Ellicott City Fire Department responded to 111 alarms, including thirty-three field fires, twenty-two dwelling or business fires, and fourteen automobile fires.

Seeking a solution to the dilemma, the Association's Board of Directors convened in special session March 25, 1954. Following an extensive discussion, the board decided to ask the County Commissioners to have two paid drivers on duty during the day, and then ask volunteer firemen to take over at night. While they negotiated with the Commissioners, the directors asked a longtime active member of the Fire Department, Mr. Charles A. Klein, and his son, Edward, to drive the engines during the day, on the understanding that they would be compensated at their regular rate of pay for whatever time they spent on fire calls. The Kleins agreed, and the arrangement proved satisfactory for the time being.

Yet the problem went deeper than a mere shortage of drivers. In the mid-1950s, suburbs of metropolitan areas across the country were expanding tremendously, and Howard County was no exception. As the county's population grew, so did the danger that residential developments might be left without adequate fire protection. Accordingly, one member of the Association's Board of Directors proposed a resolution May 27, 1954, asking the County Commissioners to investigate the possibility of a partially or fully

RESOLUTION

of the
Board of Directors of The Ellicott City
Volunteer Firemen's Association
on the death of

CHARLES PURNELL DITCH

Charles Purnell Ditch was born July 30, 1909. He joined this Department in June, 1931, and from that day until the day of his death was one of its best fire fighters and most faithful members. He soon rose to the position of Driver and Engineer, and on many occasions very capably handled this Department's equipment. He was killed in the line of duty on the morning of the recent Christmas day. He was intensely interested in all civic affairs, and devoted quite a lot of his time to activities that might benefit, or be of interest to the community. He was a devout Christian, and an ardent laborer in his church's work. He was a devoted husband and father. His achievements in this Department, and the high regard in which he was held in the community, are abundant proof of his worth and his courage. We will miss his sound counsel and his association; but the influence of his sterling character will remain with us in the coming years.

When we last saw him he was the picture of health. He was young enough to have much to live for; but with unfaltering front he faced death; with unfailing tenderness he took leave of life. Above the pain he heard the voice of God. With simple resignation he bowed to the divine decree; as gently as the morning comes, as quietly as the harvest ripens, he went to keep his tryst with his Maker. He is now beyond hearing anything we can say. It remains only for us to inscribe our estimate of his worth amongst the archives and on the records of this Department, so that future generations, for all time to come, may see—and seeing, be inspired thereby.

Therefore, be it resolved by the Board of Directors of the Ellicott City Volunteer Firemen's Association that in the said Charles Purnell Ditch's death, this Association has lost one of its most faithful members, the members thereof one of their most cherished friends, and the community one of its most useful citizens.

And be it further resolved that a copy of this resolution be published in the local newspaper, and another sent to his family.

RESOLUTION

of the
Board of Directors of The Ellicott City
Volunteer Firemen's Association
on the death of

JOSEPH A. STIGLER

Joseph A. Stigler was born December 17, 1919. He joined this Department in December, 1937, and from that time until his death was a faithful member thereof, and an indefatigable worker therein. After serving through the various grades, he was elected a Lieutenant. He was killed while fighting a fire on the morning of the recent Christmas day. He was a man of fine character, and soon attained an enviable reputation as a competent fire fighter and a good citizen. He was a devout Christian, and took a deep interest in his church, and labored constantly in furtherance of its work—an interest which could only have been prompted by the unfaltering faith that that work was calculated in some small degree, to help those less fortunate than himself. He was a devoted husband and father. His attractive personality endeared him to all who knew him.

When we know that to live is Christ, then, also, we know that to die is gain. If our sense of loss is the measure of his worth, so also is it the measure of his gain. For it is beyond peradventure that—

> *"Virtue treads paths that end not in the grave;*
> *No bar of endless night exiles the brave;*
> *And to the saner mind*
> *We rather seem the dead that stay behind."*

It is then for ourselves that we mourn, knowing our great loss, while he has ascended to his Father and to our Father, to his God and to our God.

Therefore, be it resolved by the Board of Directors of the Ellicott City Volunteer Firemen's Association that in the said Joseph A. Stigler's death, this Association has lost one of its best fire fighters, the members thereof one of their most dependable friends, and the community one of its most useful citizens.

And be it further resolved that a copy of this resolution be published in the local newspaper, and another sent to his family.

paid Fire Service.

The concept seemed to make sense, particularly since the Fire Department was taking on an expanded role in civil defense. Fears of a nuclear attack by the Soviet Union reached a peak in the mid-1950s, and the active members of the Ellicott City Fire Department found themselves participating in rescue training courses—along with numerous other men in the community—under the aegis of the Howard County Civil Defense Agency. The Association also joined with Civil Defense officials to purchase a heavy-duty rescue truck in September 1954; the truck—a Boyertown/Reo civil defense vehicle—was placed in service at the Ellicott City Fire Department September 22.

Responding to the requests for financial assistance from fire companies across Howard County, the Maryland General Assembly approved legislation in April 1955 empowering county officials to levy an annual specific district fire tax upon receiving requests from fire department officials. According to the terms of the bill, each district's fire company had to tell the county each summer how much money it would need for the ensuing calendar year; the commissioners then would establish the district fire taxes for that year, up to a rate of ten cents on every one hundred dollars of assessed valuation. (In 1955,

for instance, the Ellicott City Volunteer Firemen's Association estimated it needed approximately six thousand dollars a year to maintain its equipment, purchase insurance on the firefighters, and put funds aside for the purchase of new equipment.) Moreover, the same legislation wrote into law the annual appropriation of two thousand dollars from the county to the fire departments, which had previously been decided upon each year by the commissioners.

To further upgrade the county's fire protection service, numerous officials from the Howard County volunteer fire companies suggested that county officials study the feasibility of a central public emergency dispatching office. In the mid-1950s, each of the six fire companies in Howard County received and

Paul's Market (8210 Main Street)—1956 to 1981—William P. Corun, proprietor. Sketch Artist: Susan Jones.

handled its own calls. Since the end of World War II, they had all acquired base radio stations for their firehouses, and one or more mobile radios for their fire engines. Even though this system represented a considerable advance over the old telephone-based system, it still meant that not everyone at the station house could respond to an emergency, since there always had to be someone left behind to answer additional calls. Police calls went to either the Ellicott City Police Station or the State Police barracks at Waterloo or Pikesville, while ambulance calls could be taken at any fire or police station. According to one Fire Company official, the establishment of a central dispatching office would ensure that the appropriate type and amount of equipment would be sent to the scene of each emergency without delay, while avoiding duplication of effort or unnecessary trips into another company's territory.

Clearly the continuing growth of Howard County's population appeared to make such a centralized system a necessity. Consequently, the County Commissioners asked the president of the Howard County Volunteer Firemen's Association in August 1956 to establish a committee to develop specific recommendations for such a system. When the Association formed its committee, it selected B. H. Shipley Jr. to act as chairman.

On September 20, 1956, the committee issued its special report. It noted that the existing system contained numerous weaknesses. Among these were the necessity for volunteers to remain at or near the firehouses twenty-four hours a day; the absence of a central coordinating point with standardized procedures to receive the alarm, properly locate the fire, and promptly dispatch the designated company; lost time if the called company failed to respond to the alarm promptly or was engaged on a prior alarm; and the failure of some individuals to provide adequate or proper directions for reaching the fire. A centralized alarm dispatching system, however, would permit cooperation and coordination within the county and with other control centers in adjacent counties; alert and dispatch another company if the assigned company was delayed in responding for any reason; provide uniform telephonic fire alarm coverage; and prevent increases in insurance premiums due to the unavailability of a twenty-four-hour answering service.

Accordingly, the committee recommended that the county establish a central alarm system within Howard County. It also recommended that the system employ the most modern radio equipment available. "The radio equipment that is now installed in the fire service in Howard County has decreased cost and increased departmental efficiency," the committee insisted. "Before radio we were making many unnecessary runs. Now we call back a dispatched engine as soon as it becomes evident that it is not needed. Also, many times we are in isolated locations where telephones are several miles away. Now we are in constant touch with our local station."

It took several more years of study, negotiation, and installation work to make the system a reality. But the advent of disastrous blizzards in the winter of 1957–58 highlighted the need for a centralized system, and on April 5, 1959, the Howard County centralized emergency alarm system made its debut. Residents who needed any sort of emergency service—police, fire, ambulance, or civil defense—needed to remember only one number to call; for most areas, the number was 2121. (Clarksville, however, would not agree to using that number.) Because of the volume of calls expected from Ellicott City, the town was given a second number—2122. County residents could not, however, call the command center to learn the location of a fire. If they did, the opera-

tor had instructions to hang up on the caller. Apparently the public still had a bad habit of flocking to the scene of a fire and blocking the roads with their cars, thereby rendering the firefighters' job more difficult. The best way to prevent such obstruction, officials decided, was simply to refuse any calls about the locations of fire emergencies.

Although each locality had its own number for residents to dial, all of the numbers automatically connected to the alarm control center, located on the top floor of the Howard County Jail in Ellicott City. There, two operators would be on duty twenty-four hours a day, every day. Upon receiving calls for fire emergencies, the operator would use the selective signaling radio equipment built into the console to trigger the appropriate station siren. The operator then radioed the location and type of fire to the first man to arrive at the station. Since the old radio sets used by the fire stations and the fire engines were on a different wavelength, each station had to maintain two separate sets of radios, until they installed new radios on the same wavelength as the central alarm system during the following year.

If additional assistance was needed, the firefighters could radio the alarm center, which would immediately call out the appropriate neighboring companies. Because Howard County contains numerous deep valleys and sharp hills, the system employed a mobile repeater technique, using a repeater station located on the grounds of Howard High School, on Route 108 (8700 Old Annapolis Road), which was one of the highest points in the county. With the construction of three stations at the repeater site, including units for the police and highway systems, the system ensured full countywide emergency communications.

Each station, function, and piece of apparatus also had its own separate identification code, a combination of letters and numbers. The function letters were: "C" for Chief, "A" for ambulance, "E" for engine, "L" for ladder truck, "R" for rescue, "T" for tank truck, and "U" for utility vehicle. These letters are still used to identify equipment and personnel, except for "rescue," which is now known as "squad." Department identification numbers were: 1—Elkridge; 2—Ellicott City; 3—West Friendship; 4—Lisbon; 5—Clarksville; 6—Savage. These numbers are also still in use to identify the different fire sta-

Dedication of Howard County Central Alarm Headquarters, April 18, 1959.

tions; hence the Ellicott City Station on Main Street is known as Station 2. When the Bethany Station opened, it became known as Station 8. The third digit in the identification code pertained to a unit of function. For instance, the Elkridge Fire Department's Engine No. 2 would be identified as E-12, for "engine," "Elkridge," and "No. 2."

The system was officially dedicated April 18, 1959, in a public ceremony. By the time it was complete, the estimated cost for the entire system—the first unified, single-control electronic operation of its kind in the state of Maryland—was $36,000. Eighteen thousand dollars had been contributed by the Maryland State Civil Defense agency; the Howard County Commissioners allotted another eleven thousand dollars, while the Licensed Beverage Dealers of Howard County contributed the remaining seven thousand dollars. At the ceremony, Charles E. Delosier Jr.—who was then serving as president of the Howard County Volunteer Firemen's Association—recounted the history of the fire alarm system in Ellicott City and Howard County, from the days of the bucket brigade in 1888 to the modernized Fire Departments of 1959. "You firemen have, through their efforts, provided this county with the most modern of fire equipment and properly trained men," Delosier noted, and the central alarm system represented "a magnificent and most important milestone on the road of Progress—in the saving of lives and property in Howard County."

Certainly the pace of change throughout Ellicott City and Howard County had quickened in the postwar years. In June 1955, the Baltimore Transit Company discontinued its trolley service to Ellicott City, ending a tradition of public transportation that had lasted for more than half a century. As the county's population rose, the school system required more land and more facilities; consequently, in August 1956, the Ellicott City Volunteer Firemen's Association agreed to sell a portion of its carnival grounds to the Howard County School Board to provide space for an extension to Ellicott City Junior High School (Ellicott Mills Middle School, 4445 Montgomery Road).

The same increase in population also led the Ellicott City Volunteer Firemen's Association to inaugurate ambulance service for the first time to the residents of the Ellicott City area. Previously, the Easton's Funeral Home and the F. C. Higinbothom Funeral Home had provided ambulance service to the town, but the growing number of calls had created too much of a drain on the manpower of the businesses. When Mr. Higinbothom discontinued ambulance service in December 1957, the only public ambulance in Howard County was the one operated by the volunteer firemen in Clarksville, which was normally restricted to calls in the Fifth District.

When the Ellicott City Volunteer Firemen's Association first debated the establishment of an ambulance service, they recognized that any attempt to operate an ambulance would place a similar drain on the manpower of the Association, but they also understood that they could not simply leave the community bereft of any emergency transportation service. In January 1958, therefore, the Association's Board of Directors agreed to provide ambulance

First Ellicott City Volunteer Firemen's Association ambulance in front of Fire Station No. 2 (8390 Main Street). It was a 1953 DeSota Sedan.

service to the residents of Ellicott City and the surrounding area. They purchased the vehicle Mr. Higinbothom had been using, and outfitted it with a two-way radio, warning signals, lights and basic emergency equipment. To help defray the additional expenses of purchasing and altering the ambulance (approximately $2,500), the Association appealed to the public for contributions.

With new responsibilities and a modern, central alarm system on the way, the Ellicott City Volunteer Firemen's Association also experienced a change in leadership in 1958. After thirty-four years of dedicated service to the community, first as chief engineer of the Fire Company and then as its long-time chief, B. H. Shipley decided to retire. During the course of a remarkable career, Chief Shipley had also served as the first president of the Howard County Volunteer Firemen's Association, and as president of the Maryland State Firemen's Association and the Maryland Fire Chief's Association. At the Ellicott City Association's annual banquet December

6, 1958, Chief Shipley was presented with a special plaque in recognition of his services. He also was appointed to the honorary position of Chief Emeritus, as a tribute to the invaluable contributions he had made to Ellicott City and Howard County. His successor as chief was the Association's captain, B. H. Shipley Jr., who had himself been a member of the Ellicott City Fire Department since 1930.

Additional changes occurred in the leadership of the Association at the same time that the new chief assumed his office. For the newly created position of deputy chief, the members of the Association chose T. Woodrow Collette, who had been a member of the Fire Company since 1936. As deputy chief, Mr. Collette would be responsible for the training activities of

B. H. "Harry" Shipley holding silver plaque presented in 1958 to him and his wife, Mary J. "May" Shipley, for their more than thirty-four years of service to the Ellicott City Volunteer Firemen's Association.

the Association's active members. The new captain of the Association was Charles E. Delosier Jr.; popularly known as "Buck," Mr. Delosier had joined the Ellicott City Fire Company in 1940, and had long been active in Howard County and Maryland State Firemen's organizations. In 1958, he served as chairman of the legislative committees of both the county and state groups. As lieutenants, the Association selected Mr. Charles S. Hare, a member of the Howard County Volunteer Firemen's Association Executive Committee; Mr. James F. Eslin, a past president of the County Association; Mr. George E. Massey, a member of the Ellicott City Association since 1952.

One thing that did not change was the dedication shown by the volunteer firefighters, who continued to contribute their time and energy to the community without pay. "It is hard to assess the value of the service rendered by this department to the community in terms of cost," noted the new Chief Shipley in assessing the state of his department in December 1958. "The men in this department give their time willingly. To be in the service, they have to spend time in training, they have to answer emergency calls at any time of the day or night, they have to assist in fund-raising efforts, and they

have to like this work." So why did men still agree to volunteer? "I joined to help out," explained Charles A. Klein, one of the fire company's engineers who long had been one of its engine drivers. "I operate a garage in this community, so as a member of it, I felt it was my responsibility to do something to protect it. Back in 1941 when I joined, the department was also short on qualified engine drivers."

As Captain Delosier pointed out, the variety of requests received by the Department by the late 1950s had increased as the volume of calls rose. "For instance," he explained, "we receive calls to pump flooded basements; once in a while we get calls from people who want us to have a crew stand by while brush is burned; and we get calls from others who want us to get someone out of a locked room." By the end of 1958, the cost of operating the Fire Department had risen to between $7,000 and $8,000 per year, not counting the funds put in reserve to purchase new equipment, which still came from the proceeds of the Association's annual carnival.

Beyond the increased volume of emergency alarm calls, the congestion that arose from the residential housing boom in Howard County posed a special problem. "We are charged with protecting the life and property of several thousand people in the immediate community of Ellicott City alone," explained Chief Shipley. "The fact that everything is crowded together makes our assignment tough. When a fire hits one building, it could easily spread to another. If we don't get to a fire fast, it could cause a great deal of damage."

And, not surprisingly, the community still lacked an adequate supply of water to fight fires. The problem was especially acute in the rural areas of the Fire Department's protection zone, because there were no fire hydrants there. When the firefighters answered calls outside the city limits, they usually took about 1,300 gallons of water with them. Sometimes even that supply was inadequate, and the Department had to rely on assistance from other departments.

Within the Ellicott City limits, the problem lay in the continued presence of the old six-inch water mains, which permitted the firefighters to connect only one pumper at a time. Fortunately, plans had already been made to enhance the town's water supply by installing a series of fire hydrants along U.S. Route 40 to Rogers Avenue, which would permit Ellicott City firefighters to receive additional water from the Baltimore City system. "The additional water source was needed in order to

supply the rapidly expanding population of this area," agreed Captain Delosier. "But it's sure going to help us because fighting a fire with an inadequate water supply is a real handicap."

A fire that occurred the morning of October 26, 1958, illustrated the lengths the Ellicott City firefighters needed to go in order to fight fires outside the town limits. Shortly after dawn, the Fire Company received a call saying that there was a fire somewhere east of St. John's Lane. Upon receiving a second call that said a house was on fire in the Normandy Heights section of the county, Chief Shipley dispatched two engines. As he approached Normandy Heights, the chief was able to see the flames from a mile away, so he radioed for a third engine from Catonsville. When they arrived at the scene, there was no available supply of water, and so the firefighters used the booster tanks on their engines. After using about five hundred gallons of water to knock down the flames, they were about ready to enter the burning structure and complete the job, when the tanks ran dry.

Subsequently they had to return to Ellicott City to refill their engines—a five-mile round trip—before the fire finally could be extinguished.

During 1958, the Ellicott City Fire Department responded to a total of seventy-five alarms, including twenty-five brush and field fires, ten dwelling fires, eight chimney fires, and twelve vehicle fires. All together, the volunteer firefighters put in over 390 hours at fires, and several hundred hours more standing by at the engine house. In slightly more than nine months, the Fire Department's ambulance service answered 183 calls, requiring nearly 500 man-hours.

Before the end of the year, the Ellicott City Volunteer Firemen's Association managed to assemble sufficient supporting evidence to support its request for a district fire tax. As required by the relevant legislation, the Association had to determine how much income it would need for the following year, and submit detailed plans for its proposed expenditures.

Fortunately, the Association's long-time treasurer, Dr. Benjamin Mellor Jr., had maintained comprehensive financial records. Since Dr. Mellor and Chief Shipley knew precisely what the department needed, they were able to obtain a tax of five cents per one hundred dollars of property value from the County Commissioners without too much difficulty. Projections by Lloyd G. Taylor, the clerk of the County Commissioners, estimated that the tax would bring in at least $10,920 during 1959.

As the Association moved into 1959, it elected a slate of officers that included Dr. George B. Hansen as president, B. H. Shipley Jr. as vice president, Charles E. Delosier Jr. as secretary, and Dr. Benjamin Mellor Jr. as treasurer. Chief Shipley and Deputy Chief Collette were reelected to their respective positions, and Dr. Hansen was also elected as head of the ambulance service. During its January meeting, the Association decided to discontinue its annual carnival. Attendance at the carnival had declined in recent years, partly because other organizations had begun to sponsor similar affairs to raise funds. And with the advent of the district fire tax (which brought in more than $10,000 in 1959), the Association had less need for the carnival proceeds. In fact, the Association possessed sufficient funds to purchase a new ambulance in March 1959. Built on a 1959 Pontiac chassis, the ambulance cost approximately $9,300, and arrived at the Ellicott City Fire Station in May.

Before it arrived, however, Ellicott City suffered its most spectacular fire in more than five years. On the afternoon of March 17, a large barn on the cattle farm owned by Fred A. Kaiser, on the corner of Ridge Road off of Rogers Avenue (Ridge Road and Ellicott Center Drive) caught fire. Whipped by gusty winds, the flames quickly consumed the huge barn—which had long been a landmark for motorists on Route 40—as well as other buildings on Kaiser's farm. Although the Ellicott City firefighters arrived on the scene soon after receiving the alarm, they were again stymied by a lack of water. The firefighters expended all the water in the tanks on their truck, tapped "Pop" Buell's Pond (to the rear of 8601 Baltimore National Pike—Route 40) and set up a relay system to bring water from the hydrants on Main Street. But still it was not enough. Ironically, a brand new fire hydrant stood near the barn, on Rogers Avenue and Ridge Road, but since the water main extension had

William F. Klein, first career firefighter in Howard County's Fire Service, May 1959.

not been completed, the hydrant had not been placed into service.

In May 1959, the Fire Department employed its first full-time paid driver, William F. Klein, a volunteer member since 1949. During the meeting of the Association's Board of Directors the previous November, Chief Shipley had outlined the reasons for requesting authority to hire paid drivers. Those reasons included: a more rapid response by the Fire Department to emergencies; the growth of population in the area served by the Ellicott City Fire Department; the increasing volume of ambulance calls, particularly during weekday mornings; and the enhanced capability of a full-time employee to care for and maintain the Department's equipment. Acting on Chief Shipley's recommendation, the Fire Department hired Mr. Klein to start work May 4, 1959. On January 1, 1960, the Department added a part-time paid driver, Mr. Frederick A. Richards, a volunteer since 1947.

The following year, Ellicott City's Fire Department logged a total of 112 fire alarms, a considerable increase over the previous years. Again the highest category was brush, field, and woods fires (thirty-

three), with dwelling (twenty-two), vehicle (fourteen), and chimney fires (twelve) close behind. The Department put in a total of 886 man-hours in responding to fire emergencies; interestingly, the vast majority of fire alarms came between noon and five o'clock in the afternoon.

Log cabin along Cat Rocks Stream, "Missionary Bottom," Merryman Street.

Rear view of Tongue Row, Old Columbia Pike.

SEVEN
1960-1997

During 1960, the Ellicott City Volunteer Firemen's Association continued its intensive training and public education programs. Its members attended forty-six firefighting training sessions, and seventeen members of the Fire Department received certificates from the University of Maryland for completing its Fire Service Extension course. The Department also distributed fire prevention literature to all the schools in the area—including Howard High, Ellicott City Junior High, Ellicott City Elementary, St. John's Lane Elementary, Fel's Lane Elementary, and St. Paul's Parochial—and gave lectures and demonstrations to schools and cub scout/boy scout groups as well. Just as important, the Department also conducted a series of fire inspections to Ellicott City's public and private schools. To enhance its efficiency in

responding to both fire and ambulance emergency calls, the Association appointed a second full-time paid driver in 1960, and established a program of preventive maintenance for its apparatus and equipment. The only major fire that occurred during the year was one of the most tragic in recent times, when a two-year-old child suffocated in an attic fire in a home on Fel's Lane (Parking Lot F); as far as investigators could determine, the fire was started by children playing with matches.

In an effort to alleviate the long-standing shortage of public water in the Ellicott City area, particularly in the sections that had experienced significant residential and commercial growth, county officials approved, in February 1961, a plan to extend the town's water mains. Meanwhile, Howard County had expanded its central alarm system by constructing a 300-foot-tall transmitting tower, which allowed it to broadcast and receive radio signals from nearly every part of central Maryland. The system was successfully handling all calls to the county's fire, police, and ambulance services, as well as the sheriff's office, the roads department, and the Howard County Civil Defense agency. So valuable was its contribution to the area's safety that the chief dispatcher, William W. Boyd, was promoted. And officials from other counties were making a pilgrimage to Ellicott City to inspect the system in operation, in hopes of developing similar systems of their own. In fact, one visitor from the town of Keene, New Hampshire, stated unequivocally that Howard County officials had "accomplished more, dollar for dollar, in affording your surrounding area with a modern emergency communication service than any other installation which I have visited. . . . It is clearly obvious to me that your group has

spent a lot of time and planning in an entirely unselfish and dedicated manner," he concluded, "which I hope your citizens appreciate."

Like his father, Chief Shipley enthusiastically promoted fire safety education programs, and he dispatched complete kits of fire prevention materials to all the schools in the Second District. Remembering the numerous fires that had struck Ellicott City's churches over the years, Chief Shipley also sought to launch a fire evacuation program in every church in his company's district. Accordingly, the Ellicott City Fire Department sent evacuation bulletins to every church in the area in September 1961. And to further improve their ability to respond to emergencies, the Ellicott City Volunteer Firemen's Association purchased an American LaFrance "900 Deluxe Invader" triple combination pumper in October 1961. The new engine, which cost $26,950, had the capability of pumping 750 gallons per minute, and included chemical extinguishers, 1,200 feet of $2^{1/2}$ inch hose, 500 feet of $1^{1/2}$ inch hose, a generator, a 500-gallon booster tank, and a deluge set for major fires. It could carry as many as ten men, if necessary. When the new engine arrived, the venerable 1929 American LaFrance pumper was officially retired from first-line service.

Training evolutions. Captain Charles E. Delosier Jr. leaning on fence, circa 1961.

Despite the best efforts of the Association, however, the frequency of alarms continued to increase. The only serious fire of 1962 was a blaze in a duplex dwelling at 303–305 Main Street (8505–8507 Frederick Road), but during the twelve-month period, the Ellicott City Fire Company responded to 428 emergency calls—both fire and ambulance combined. Consequently, the company found it necessary to add a third full-time paid firefighter to its staff; the following year, a fourth full-time firefighter was added, along with one part-time employee to serve as an ambulance driver on weekdays.

Obviously, the use of paid employees led to a significant increase in the Fire Department's budget; for the first six months of 1964, the Department estimated that it would need $15,900 in operating expenses.

The central alarm system also continued to expand its capabilities, while repeatedly demonstrating its usefulness to the county. During the winter of 1961–62, a house in the Lisbon area caught fire during a heavy snowfall when many roads in the western section of the county were blocked. Because of the coordination afforded by the system, the central dispatcher was able to alert the highways department, which sent a snowplow to the scene to open the road so that the firefighters' engines could get to the fire quickly. In a similar manner, the system was able to serve as a communications center and coordinate the rescue efforts of numerous county agencies when an airliner crashed into a Howard County farm near Clarksville in December 1962.

So proud were the county's fire companies of their role in developing the central alarm system that they reacted with undisguised anger when the County Commissioners proposed in January 1963 to turn over operating control of the system to the county's police department. In effect, Central Alarm personnel would be merged into the police department, and would even wear police uniforms. The commissioners' rationale was that the system was used principally by the police, and that the move would improve the quality of the county's police services, which apparently had been lagging behind the fire services, in part due to a rapid turnover in personnel at the top. The Howard County Police Station (8316 Main Street) still did not operate on a twenty-four-hour basis in early 1963, a situation which the consolidation of the police department and the command center would remedy.

The commissioners had failed to notify either the county's fire departments or civil defense officials of the proposed transfer, however. On February

3, the Howard County Volunteer Firemen's Association voted unanimously to oppose and protest the commissioners' move. In a telegram to the commissioners, the Association noted that "it is the considered opinion of the Howard County Volunteer Firemen's Association that the function of Central Alarm should be of an independent communications operation and not under the supervision of any one particular department using its services." Another Association spokesman explained that the firefighters were especially upset because they had obtained a large portion of the original funding for the system, "and then this was done suddenly without even the courtesy of a call to fire department heads."

So vociferous was the opposition of the fire companies, supported by civil defense officials, that the commissioners soon backed down. After meeting with representatives from the Firemen's Association, the commissioners announced that the system would continue operating as a separate agency, responsible only to the commissioners themselves. "Our main purpose," stated Commissioner David W. Force, "is to have cooperation between all those who use the system."

As the controversy over the central alarm system moved toward its resolu-

tion, the county firemen pressed forward on another front—the adoption of a uniform building code "with teeth in it." Even though residential construction had been increasing rapidly in Howard County, the government still possessed no enforceable code of its own, and had to rely instead upon codes established by the Maryland State Government and other localities, such as Prince George's County. The absence of adequate enforcement authority especially concerned the county's firefighters, who urged the county to adopt a code "so that the fire marshals can correct dangerous situations," such as those that allegedly had caused the death of two children in a Marriottsville wooden frame dwelling in February 1963.

In response, the General Assembly's Committee on Fire Codes, headed by Howard County's Senator James Clark Jr., strongly urged in December 1963 that the state adopt a uniform minimum fire code. By the spring of 1964, Howard County officials were preparing to develop the county's first housing code for rental buildings. Representatives from the Fire Department, the Planning Department, the Zoning Commissioner's Office, and the Office of the Building Engineer received training from an official of the State Health Department, using the standards established by the United States Public

Health Service to ensure that county structures met a minimum level of safety and hygiene. The Fire Department's representative was Chief Shipley himself, who subsequently served as assistant administrator for the Housing Division of Howard County from 1964 to 1966.

Fatal house fire, four deaths—February 25, 1965.

Unfortunately, the implementation of Howard County's new housing code in March 1965 came too late to save a family that perished in a tragic fire on Fel's Lane February 25, 1965. Just as the Board of County Commissioners was preparing to purchase and raze a fifty-three-acre section of substandard housing in the Fel's Lane area, a fire erupted at a rental property at 26 Fel's Lane (Parking Lot F). Apparently the blaze

began when spilled kerosene around a heating stove caught fire. The father of the family managed to save one child and attempted to save his wife and three other children, but the flames spread too quickly through the building. All four victims retreated to the third floor, but the building lacked any secondary means of escape from the upper floor. Since the house was only yards away from the Ellicott City Fire Station, the firefighters arrived within several minutes of receiving the call, but the call itself had been delayed because the house had no telephone.

The tragic incident highlighted the need for the sort of fire prevention measures long advocated by officials of the Ellicott City Volunteer Firemen's Association. The responsibilities of the Association now extended far beyond fighting fires, and its duties would continue to expand in various ways in the future as the county's population increased, and Howard County made the transition from a rural community to a suburban one. The key to the continued efficiency of the Department, Chief Shipley believed, was orderly, coordinated planning. "The time has arrived for us to realize we must plan and be prepared to increase our overall operations in an orderly and progressive manner as our community grows, and not suddenly be confronted with a crash program," he wrote in January 1964. "Estimating and forecasting our responsibilities will aid greatly in the future for an efficient fire department."

The counsel to the county's Planning Commission agreed. "We must evaluate the means and methods whereby the same high level of fire protection may be expanded to a growing community," noted Robert E. Wieder in a letter to the County Commissioners in February 1964, and he suggested that representatives of the six volunteer fire companies meet with the commissioners to coordinate plans for the expansion of fire protection service.

An example of the Fire Department's growing role within the community arose in late 1965, when Chief Shipley urged the Howard County Planning Commission to consider fire and rescue problems before approving any rental housing projects in the future. In particular, Chief Shipley was concerned about plans to construct garden-type apartment houses on Court House Drive. Such a structure would require the Department to purchase a ladder truck—an issue the Firemen's Association had already discussed earlier that year—and would necessitate adequate level space around the apartments to park the ladder truck and raise its ladders.

And again Chief Shipley called for improved planning and training within the Fire Department to handle the increasing demands. "We can expect serious problems with expansion in the second district," he wrote in January 1966. "There is going to be a population increase with the rapid development of homes, apartment buildings, schools, together with an increase in commercial buildings. The influx of people and activity are going to create new and added hazards and double the burden of our fire department. To meet the demands that will be placed upon us, it will be necessary to place emphasis on training and molding our manpower into a well-organized team. . . . I cannot over emphasize the urgency that is required of us to meet the problems that will be confronting us."

Chief Shipley also urged the County Commissioners to look toward the future by coordinating the county's fire service activities—such as fire prevention, inspections, and investigations—and by coordinating the administrative interaction of the Fire Department with other county agencies, including the Board of Education, Housing Administrator, Planning Commission, Zoning Commission, and the Police Department. To facilitate precisely this sort of coordination, the Board of County

Commissioners created the new post of Fire Coordinator, and appointed Chief Shipley to fill the position. Chief Shipley had, in fact, been recommended to the post by the county's six fire companies, who greeted his appointment with approbation.

At this point, Mr. Shipley was actually wearing three hats—Chief of the Ellicott City Volunteer Fire Department, Deputy County Housing Administrator, and County Fire Coordinator. In his newest role, Mr. Shipley had the responsibility of working with the county's six fire companies and the Maryland Rating Bureau to complete a survey of the county's fire protection needs, including manpower (county officials were becoming resigned to the necessity of additional full-time, paid firemen), the purchase of new equipment, and location of future fire stations. The end result was a comprehensive list of recommendations designed to help county officials cope with the sort of accelerated growth Howard County had been experiencing.

Even Main Street in Ellicott City, with its venerable buildings and time-honored traditions, was showing the effects of growth and change. In the autumn of 1964, the Howard County Roads Department tore down the filling station that had long stood at the cor-

ner of Columbia Pike and Main Street, to widen the intersection and enable cars to turn onto either thoroughfare with much greater ease. (Previously, motorists who wanted to turn onto Main Street had to pull far to the left when exiting from Columbia Pike, creating a perennial traffic bottleneck.) As one observer pointed out, school bus drivers were particularly pleased with this improvement.

Another significant step toward modernization occurred in May 1965, when the County Commissioners voted to install special emergency telephones at six strategic locations in Ellicott City: at 28 Main Street (8044 Main Street), 83 Main Street (8133 Main Street), Main Street & Church Road, 272 West Main Street (8472 Frederick Road), 37 Fel's Lane (Parking Lot F), and St. Paul Street & New Cut Road. Installed by Central Alarm and the Bell Telephone System, the telephones automatically connected a caller with the switchboard at central alarm headquarters atop the county jail. The caller would then identify the nature of the emergency, and the central alarm dispatcher would notify the appropriate agency. (The calls would also be automatically taped, to discourage false alarms.) Officials hoped that the use of such phones, particularly in areas of minimal telephone service,

Howard County's first courthouse on Mercer Street (parking lot F), originally scheduled for demolition as part of Howard County's 1969 Hilltop Urban Renewal Program. The structure has been preserved.

Emporium, located at 2 Main Street (8000 Main Street). Once again, the old water mains along Main Street—the legacy of the old Maryland Water Works Company—proved inadequate, and only the use of Patapsco River water saved the lower end of town from complete destruction.

Slightly more than a year later, January 16, 1965, a more destructive fire demolished a row of buildings at 37–49 Main Street (8059–8069 Main Street), including a billiards hall, a doctor's office, a cleaner, and a laundry center. Moreover, the third floor of Easton's Funeral Home suffered extensive damage. Ironically, the same buildings had been burned down once before, on New Year's Eve, 1941. As a result of this latest conflagration, seventeen adults and three children—who lived above the shops and offices—were left homeless.

Two more fires caused extensive property damage in 1966. On the evening of March 17, a woodworking shop and storage area owned by Crain

would help prevent such tragedies as the February 1965 fire on Fel's Lane. Within a year, officials of the Ellicott City Volunteer Firemen's Association were petitioning the County Commissioners to expand the emergency phone service by installing additional telephones

Beyond the Fel's Lane fire, there had been several serious fires in downtown Ellicott City in the early 1960s. On December 29, 1963, flames struck two buildings—the Edward T. Clark and Son's Lawn Mower Sales and Service, and the historic stone building previously known as Radcliff's Old

Laminates, Inc., at 8¹/² Columbia Pike (3709 Old Columbia Pike) caught fire, destroying nearly all the cabinets and kitchen work tops in the building, along with stores of plywood, packing boxes, corrugated paper, and similarly inflammable material. And on July 16, flames destroyed the interior of a two-story frame house at 3765 Church Road. No lives were lost in either fire, although several volunteer firefighters received minor injuries in battling the blaze on Columbia Pike.

By 1967, the first residences and commercial buildings of the new town of Columbia, designed and supervised by the Rouse Company and financed largely by the Connecticut General Insurance Company, had begun to emerge on the west side of Route 29, south of Route 108. The advent of Columbia, along with the increase in residential and commercial construction in Ellicott City, posed a host of challenges for Howard County officials. To grasp the magnitude of the problems facing county officials, the second district alone—in and around Ellicott City—had added 2,555 new dwellings between 1958 and 1968, along with 87 commercial buildings, 364 apartment units, and 367 miscellaneous buildings. By 1970, experts predicted that the population of the second district would reach 25,000.

Obviously county officials needed to provide adequate fire protection for all of Howard County's new residents, including the citizens of Columbia. During 1966 and 1967, Fire Department officials repeatedly advised the Board of County Commissioners that it would need to organize at least six or seven additional engine companies in the areas of intensive population growth. Many experts—including members of the Ellicott City Volunteer Firemen's Association—also recommended that the Ellicott City Fire Department form a ladder company, which obviously would require the purchase of a truck having at least an eighty-five-foot aerial ladder. Since ladder trucks did not come cheaply—the estimated cost ran

Enclosing a section of the Hudson Branch in the 8400 Block of Frederick Road—a part of Howard County's 1969 Hilltop Urban Renewal Program. The branch was rerouted to save razing the County's first courthouse.

between $60,000 and $100,000, the issue of financing proved a particularly sticky one. In early April 1968, the commissioners finally approved the purchase of a ladder truck, but local banks adamantly refused to loan the necessary funds to the Ellicott City Fire Department.

After several weeks of negotiation, the commissioners agreed to finance the ladder truck with funds from the following year's general budget, and specifically from the Second District's fire tax revenues. That decision was later amended, as the commissioners decided to fund the ladder truck with revenue from the recordation and property

Howard County's first rear mount one-hundred-foot aerial ladder truck—placed in service April 16, 1970. First Fire Department apparatus purchased using recordation transfer tax funds.

transfer taxes. Fire Department personnel originally had intended to purchase a ladder truck with a tiller, where a driver rode in the back to steer; if they had gone ahead with this concept, they would have had to build an addition to the fire station to house the truck. Just at that time, however, American LaFrance came through with a demonstration model of a ladder truck they had built for the fire department of Gary, Indiana. On this model, the base of the ladder was mounted to the rear of the truck.

Unlike the tiller type of ladder truck, this vehicle would fit comfortably inside the existing station. On April 16, 1970, therefore, the Ellicott City Fire Department put into service an American LaFrance "Ladder Chief" rear mount, one-hundred-foot aerial ladder truck. The ladder truck was subsequently made available for fires throughout Howard County, including Columbia—where the advent of high-rise apartments made it invaluable—but it was

officially assigned to the Ellicott City Fire Department, because that department had the largest number of paid personnel (four) and the highest assessable tax base to generate revenue from the district fire tax. The truck was designed so that it could be operated by four firefighters, but Chief Shipley made it clear that he would prefer at least seven firefighters go out with the truck on each emergency call.

Meanwhile, fire emergency calls continued to rise, as did requests for ambulance service. In 1967, the Ellicott City Fire Department responded to 276 fires, and more than 500 ambulance calls. Fortunately, the number of volunteers also had increased to forty-two (of whom twenty-five were active members), and Chief Shipley made certain they received adequate training. Ellicott City firefighters continued to attend the twenty-week training courses sponsored by the University of Maryland Extension Service, but Chief Shipley and his colleagues also staged their own training sessions.

In March 1968, the Howard County Volunteer Firemen's Association, under the direction of Chief Shipley, inaugurated a countywide training program for its firefighters. Whenever possible, Chief Shipley employed a dilapidated, unwanted building for his training program, setting fires in one part of the structure so his men could learn the fundamentals of firefighting under realistic, simulated conditions. In the spring and summer of 1972, for instance, the Ellicott City Fire Department used the old Shaffer Convalescent Home on Montgomery Road for practice. The owners of the property had wanted to raze the building because it had suffered repeated attacks from vandals in recent years; at their request, Shipley gradually burned out the interior of the structure in a series of firefighting exercises. Later the owners, Long Gate Ventures Inc., brought in bulldozers to knock down the foot-thick walls. The site later became part of the Long Gate shopping complex, housing a Target department store, Safeway, Barnes & Noble bookstore, and other commercial ventures. After selling a part of their former carnival grounds on the other side of Montgomery Road to the Young Men's Christian Association of the Greater Baltimore Area in September 1970, the firefighters also helped the YMCA demolish and remove three old buildings on that parcel as part of another series of training exercises.

During the late 1960s and early 1970s, the membership of the Ellicott City Volunteer Firemen's Association was changing as well. As will be seen below, the ranks of paid firefighters were steadily growing, and in November 1968, the Association voted—in a near-unanimous ballot—to admit the first black firefighter to its ranks. The new member, forty-two-year-old Mr. Joseph M. Fuller, stated that he had "always wanted to be a fireman," ever since he was a boy growing up in Ellicott City, watching the shiny red fire trucks rushing off to answer alarms. He claimed that he received no special treatment from his fellow firefighters. "They treat me as an individual regardless of my color," he said, "and make me feel no different from anybody else. It's really a pleasure to be out there with the boys." As far as Chief Shipley was concerned, Mr. Fuller was just like any other firefighter. "He really is a hard worker," he noted. "No one can say he doesn't hold up his own end." The first female firefighter in Ellicott City, Martha A. Trollinger, joined the Fire Department June 26, 1974, and served until October 27, 1976.

As the Association entered new territory in the rapidly changing Howard County environment in the late 1960s, it also paused to honor its past. In June 1967, a representative of the Ellicott City Volunteer Firemen's Association asked the Board of County Commissioners to consider establishing a Fire

Department museum on the site of the original fire station house, at the corner of Main Street and Ellicott Street (now Church Road). Since it had been purchased by the county several decades earlier, the site had been used as a library annex and county office building. Most recently, it had housed the county's sanitation office. But since that office had relocated, the Association broached the possibility of returning the site "to something near its original use." The proposal to devote a building to a significant aspect of Howard County's history seemed particularly appropriate, since the town was beginning to experience a renaissance with the restoration of other historical sites and the establishment of upscale shops with a sort of quaint, nineteenth-century charm. It would take another several decades to bring this project to completion.

In the meantime, Ellicott City lost a valued member of its community when Fire Chief Emeritus B. H. Shipley passed away September 25, 1967. In the years following his retirement from active duty with the Fire Department, Mr. Shipley had accepted a position as a committing magistrate for Howard County. Then, when the People's Court came into existence in 1964, he was appointed to serve as the court's first bailiff. Beyond the vital work he had performed for the Fire Department, Mr. Shipley had been active in the town's fraternal organizations. He was one of the founders of the Ellicott City Lion's Club, and served as the club's first president in 1948; he had also been a member of the Knights of Pythias; the Patmos Lodge, Masonic Order; and Center Lodge 40, Centre Encampment 31, and Naomi Rebekah Lodge of the Odd Fellows.

In Mr. Shipley's honor, the Howard County Volunteer Firemen's Association held a special memorial service October 19, to allow its members to pay their respects to the first president of the Association. As Paul F. J. LePore, then president of the Association, explained to the rest of the community, "Only we, the members of the Howard County Volunteer Fire Service, know the many personal sacrifices required of Chief Shipley over a long and dedicated period of faithful volunteer service to the county and its people."

Certainly Mr. Shipley would have been proud to know that his son was appointed by the County Commissioners in September 1968 to serve as Howard County's first part-time Fire Administrator. The Commissioners had been considering hiring a "fire co-ordinator-administrator" since earlier in the year, to help coordinate the efforts of the county's existing volunteer companies, and assist in the establishment of new fire stations. Given his vast experience with the Ellicott City and Howard County Volunteer Firemen's Associations, Chief Shipley clearly seemed to be "the best qualified man" for the position, as one county commissioner appropriately described him.

In his new role, Chief Shipley also served as a direct liaison between the Commissioners and the Fire Advisory Board, and he continued to play an integral role in fire inspection of buildings. He also acted as a troubleshooter when problems arose in recruiting personnel for the command center, or purchasing new emergency equipment. Since 1954, Chief Shipley had been serving on the Board of Trustees of the Maryland State Firemen's Association (including a stint as chairman of the Board), but his increasing responsibilities in Howard County required him to reduce his commitments to the state organization. When Howard County voters adopted the charter system of government, the county's first executive, Omar J. Jones, continued Chief Shipley's appointment as Fire Administrator. In March 1970, Executive Jones added to Mr. Shipley's responsibilities when he made the County Fire Administrator responsible for the direct supervision of the central alarm system.

When Executive Jones made the position of Fire Administrator a full-time position in July 1971, he chose another experienced Fire Department executive to the post. Less than a year later, however, Executive Jones selected Chief Shipley to serve Howard County in yet another capacity, as the county's representative on the Regional Planning Council's Emergency Medical Services Committee. In the summer of 1973, Mr. Jones appointed Chief Shipley to be the county executive's personal representative on the Board of Directors to the Emergency Medical Services Development, Inc., of the Regional Planning Council.

During the late 1960s, while Ellicott City was experiencing all the pangs of sudden population growth wrought by the birth of the new Columbia, Ellicott City suffered only one major fire. On February 13, 1969, the administration building of Taylor Manor Hospital—located at 4110 College Avenue—went up in flames. The main building of the hospital, a successor to the former Patapsco Manor Sanitarium, housed more than two dozen patients and all the hospital's office facilities. The fire, which apparently began in a storage room, was discovered shortly before 2:30 in the afternoon. The flames quickly spread upward throughout the twenty-five-year-old structure, and soon reached the attic of the building. When the Ellicott City firefighters arrived, they had to break down the outer walls of the building with axes so they could direct streams of water directly onto the flames. A two-engine relay setup pumped water from the stream at 4194 New Cut Road. It was a particularly difficult job in the sub-freezing weather, with smoke and heat pouring from the administration building; indeed, it took fifty firefighters—including companies from Elkridge, Catonsville, Clarksville, and West Friendship—nearly three hours to quell the blaze. In the end, the firemen managed to contain the blaze, limiting the fire damage to the center section of the building. No patients were injured during the incident.

An equally dangerous fire struck Main Street on the afternoon of May 25, 1972, when flames broke out in the upper level of the historic four-story building formerly known as the Walker-Chandler House, located at 8180 Main Street, formerly 106 Main Street. (Constructed in 1790, the Walker-Chandler House had been the first duplex building in Howard County; the Walker family lived in one half of the house, and the Chandlers in the other.)

Aerial view looking east from 8390 Main Street. General area of the Howard County Courthouse and Main Street, circa 1970.

At that time, most of the building was occupied by an antique shop, Ellicott's Country Store. On the top floor, however, an elderly gentleman lived in a single apartment. As soon as neighbors across the street realized the structure was on fire, one of the shop's owners rushed into the building and, with the help of several of her friends, helped the ninety-year-old gentleman down the stairs to safety.

Arriving with the ladder truck and pumper engines, firefighters used axes to chop holes through the asphalt-shingled roof of the store (the asphalt had, of course, fed the flames in the first place) and the tin roof of the building next door to gain access to the fire. Although it took two hours to quell the flames, most of the building was saved, with damage only to the roof and several of the eighteenth-century pine beams. The building next door, at 8186 Main

Aerial view looking east from 8358 Main Street. General area of the Howard County Courthouse and Main Street, circa 1970.

Street, also suffered minor damage.

Several months later, Ellicott City experienced one of the worst floods in the history of the town with the arrival of Tropical Storm Agnes. From June 21 to 28, Ellicott City and Howard County were deluged by extraordinarily heavy rains and the consequent flooding of the Patapsco, Patuxent, and Little Patuxent Rivers to record levels. All the normal functions of local government were interrupted, as were vital public utilities. "It was a time of havoc and devastation seldom witnessed in a lifetime," recalled one observer in the immediate aftermath of the storm.

During the height of the flooding, the firefighters of the Ellicott City Fire Department provided a host of emergency services to local residents. As the waters rose ominously, the firefighters

From railroad bridge looking east. Water and debris flowing over Patapsco River Bridge connecting Baltimore and Howard Counties, caused by Tropical Storm Agnes June 1972.

Top Right: Main Street and Maryland Avenue. Flooding caused by Tropical Storm Agnes June 1972.

Looking east from 8155 Main Street. Flooding conditions caused by Tropical Storm Agnes, June 1972. Note on left, near pole, one of Ellicott City's original parking meters.

assisted with the evacuation of numerous individuals along Main Street and Frederick Road, including one female resident who adamantly refused to leave her dwelling until the fire personnel insisted. When the town's normal electrical power went off, the fire company provided emergency electrical power (including floodlights along Lower Main Street) with a standby generator. They responded to numerous requests for emergency ambulance service, responded to fire alarms—including a blaze in the Marriottsville post office—and, as the floodwaters receded, used the Department's submersible pump to remove water from the basements of a host of commercial buildings, including Commercial & Farmers Bank and Caplan's Department Store, as well as several private residences. "Perhaps we can all take a lesson in efficiency from the Volunteer Fire Service who responded so quickly and effectively to the crisis," observed County Executive Jones in a letter to Chief Shipley after the storm had passed. "It is well known that through County-wide effort and outstanding leadership and performance, the fire service stood out as a stabilizing influence over panic and hysteria. The Chief Officers, their staff and firefighter personnel, both volunteer and career, joined together in a masterful rescue and assistance effort that will long be remembered."

To help alleviate the financial pressures on the county's fire services, Chief Shipley had recommended in January 1971 that the existing fire tax districts be eliminated, and that the government substitute instead an urban fire tax district for the first, second, and sixth districts, along with the Columbia area of the fifth district. The remaining portions of the county would be amalgamated into a rural fire tax district. This program would enable the county to establish tax rates based on the total budgetary needs of all volunteer departments and county-operated fire stations, Shipley explained. Moreover, he suggested that the county implement a countywide fire tax of one cent per one hundred dollars of valued property, to provide for fire administration and training services on a countywide basis. Although it took several years for county officials to discern the wisdom and efficacy of Chief Shipley's recommendations, the County Council finally approved legislation in 1995 to establish a two-tiered urban and rural fire tax system.

Throughout the early 1970s, the Ellicott City Fire Department continued to add to its staff of full-time, career personnel. By 1975, sixteen years after the Department hired its first career firefighter, the number of career firefighters had increased to eighteen. The addition of paid staff, plus the effects of a growing county population, the expansion of fire prevention activities,

and the ravages of inflation, forced the Department's expenses to rise significantly. In 1973, the Ellicott City station responded to 310 fire alarms, plus more than 750 ambulance calls. Similar problems beset Howard County's other fire companies.

Meanwhile, the Ellicott City Fire Department was undergoing significant changes of its own. On July 1, 1974, the Department officially opened its second station, known as Bethany Fire Station No. 8, located at 9601 Route 99 in Ellicott City. Dedicated to the memory of Mr. Edward T. Clark Jr., former president of the Ellicott City Volunteer Firemen's Association, the station was operated by the Association with the same blend of volunteer and career personnel as the Main Street station.

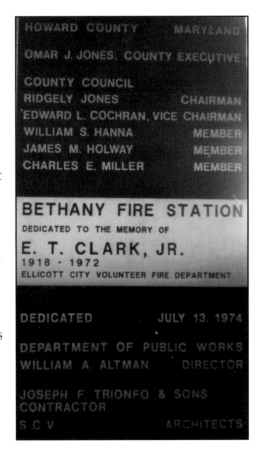

Bethany Fire Station No. 8, Route 99 and Old St. John's Lane, was dedicated in memory of E. T. Clark Jr., who at the time of his death March 29, 1972, was serving as president, Ellicott City Volunteer Firemen's Association.

While Chief Shipley supervised the operation of both stations, he delegated a certain degree of day-to-day leadership

Dedication of Bethany Fire Station No. 8, Route 99 and Old St. John's Lane, July 13, 1974. Luncheon served by the Ladies Auxiliary to the Ellicott City Volunteer Firemen's Association.

to his subordinate, Captain Henry L. Long III.

Although property owners in the Bethany-Mount Hebron area undoubtedly were grateful for the opening of a fire station in such close proximity, a number of residents complained about the station's use of the fire siren to signal emergencies. The residents of Main Street had long been accustomed to the sound of a siren, but their counterparts in the Bethany area found the siren intrusive. Although the County Council refused to prohibit the use of the siren, Chief Shipley decided to defer to the wishes of the local residents, and accordingly discontinued the use of the siren June 1, 1975. In the interest of consistency, Chief Shipley also eliminated the siren at the Main Street Station. From that time on, volunteers would be summoned by the use of radio monitors. "The discontinuance of the

siren will result in the slower response time by volunteers," Chief Shipley predicted. "The volunteers will be away from their radio monitors at times, and it will cause some delay. But if that is what the general public wants, it is what they will get," he added resignedly.

As the Ellicott City Volunteer Firemen's Association headed into the mid-1970s, its roll of officers expanded to meet the organization's increased responsibilities. At the Association's annual meeting in 1975, the active members elected Charles E. Delosier Jr. as their president; Dr. Benjamin Mellor Jr. as vice president; William E. Pfeiffer Jr. as secretary and George M. Cullum as treasurer. Chief Shipley retained his post, of course; to assist him, Charles E. Delosier Jr. was named deputy chief, and George E. Massey became battalion chief. The two captains were Henry L. Long III and Howard J. Massey III. The Association also named three lieutenants: John J. Klein, whose father, Charles, served in the Association for forty years; Charles A. Massey, and Thomas F. Merson.

The Association also was constantly upgrading its equipment. In November 1973, it added an American LaFrance "Pace Maker" one thousand-gallon per minute triple combination pumper, which was subsequently transferred to

Fire Station No. 8 when that station opened the following summer. Using funds donated by the Ellicott City Lions Club, the Association placed into service in May 1975 a sixteen-foot aluminum boat with a twenty-five-horse-power motor. The purchase of a boat seemed especially prescient in the autumn of that year, when rains from Hurricane Eloise led to the Patapsco River once more overflowing its banks. The bridge at the lower end of Main Street, which had been built when Tropical Storm Agnes destroyed the old bridge, was completely covered by the floodwaters, but ultimately managed to withstand the pressure, even though the approaches to the bridge were badly damaged. Once again the firefighters assisted both in the evacuation of residents from Main Street, and with the cleanup operations that followed the storm.

The following year, the Association used funds from the county capital budget program to obtain a 1976 American LaFrance "Century" one thousand-gallon per minute pumper for Fire Station No. 2. But the most engaging addition to the station house was a white and black Dalmatian named "Yogi." In the early 1970s, whenever the fire apparatus was leaving the Main Street firehouse, people would see "Yogi." He knew the radio tone alert signal as well as any Fire Department member, and took delight in being on the fire engine ready to respond before they were.

Yogi was about six months old when the career firefighters decided he would be their mascot and friend. He rode on the hood over the motor, behind the cab with his head high, facing the wind and barking. At the scene of a call, he would remain on the apparatus as a guard. A special lined coat of yellow canvas was made for him by the C. R. Daniels Company. During inclement weather, the coat was put on him when the engine left the firehouse. Attached to the coat were his mask and air bottle. School children would come by bus to see the firehouse mascot. Most of the time he would be very friendly, but occasionally he would leave and go off by himself.

Many visitors came to Ellicott City in 1972 for the Bicentennial Celebration. During the parades, Yogi rode standing on the front seat of the Scout Brush unit, with his front feet on top of the windshield. You would hear people shouting out, "Here comes Yogi." As the fire engine responded to an alarm on Manordale Road one day, Yogi top-

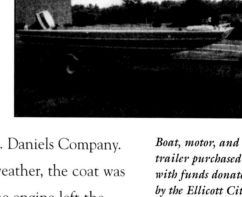

Boat, motor, and trailer purchased with funds donated by the Ellicott City Lions Club.

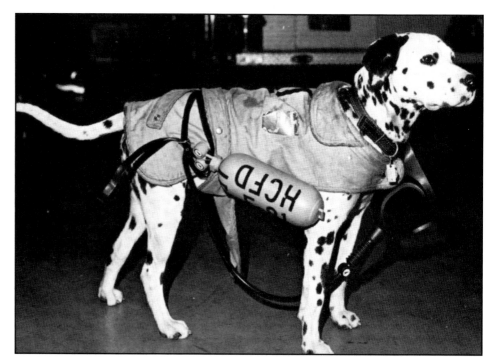

Fire dog "Yogi" wearing his yellow coat, mascot at Ellicott City Fire Station No. 2, 8390 Main Street.

Fire dogs. "Yogi" (left), mascot at Ellicott City Fire Station No. 2, 8390 Main Street. "JR," (right), mascot at Bethany Fire Station No. 8, Route 99 and Old St. John's Lane.

pled from his perch when the engine turned off St. John's Lane. He was not hurt and waited for the engine to return and pick him up. After that, he only rode with a leash on.

One day, Yogi disappeared. No one had any idea where he had gone. He had a "girlfriend" in the neighborhood and would go there to visit, but he was not there. One morning over a week later, he was waiting at the front door of the firehouse with the pads on all four feet raw. It was assumed that someone picked him up in an automobile and that he was able to free himself and return home.

In early October 1976, while following the firefighters across Main Street to the Annex, Yogi was struck by an automobile. Doctor Stuart L. Myers treated him for his injuries. People called his office inquiring about "Yogi." Many cards, telephone calls, and expressions of concern were received at the firehouse. Yogi wasn't off duty too long, and was soon back riding on the engine.

When the firefighters noticed that Yogi was not being as friendly to people as he had been, the decision was made to find another home for him. A family member of a career firefighter made a nice home for him until he died. Yogi had several offspring. One was a puppy resembling the Main Street firehouse

mascot. The personnel at the Bethany Station decided to take him, and gave him the name of JR. JR decided he would roam the neighborhood for hours. This did not create good public relations. For a while he was kept chained, but it was felt that this was not fair to him. A career firefighter agreed to provide him a good home. It didn't take long for JR to become a good family pet.

The yellow canvas coat made for Yogi was not the only apparel ever donated to the Ellicott City Fire Department by the C. R. Daniels Company. Through the generosity of Mr. Vernon T. Abel, a former director of the Ellicott City Volunteer Firemen's Association, the company has provided the Department with canvas salvage covers and other items. Just recently they provided the cover for the 1929 engine.

The community around the Daniels Mill, located several miles north of the Dickey Mills on the west side of the Patapsco River, had three names prior to the 1940s. In 1833 it was known as O'Kisco Flouring Mill and in 1845 it was known as Elysville Cotton Mill. In 1890 it became known as Alberton Cotton Mills, a town that had a cotton mill, company store, U.S. Post Office, a church, and housing for employees who

Daniels Community Band.

time Tropical Storm Agnes flooded the mill in the summer of 1972, there were only about 325 workers left. During the storm, the floodwaters of the Patapsco reached as high as forty feet over the second-floor level, and the mill never reopened. The September 17, 1977, fire represented the coup de grâce, destroying most of the old mill buildings that remained. Unfortunately, firefighters had to carry their equipment to the scene of the fire by hand, over the hills and railroad tracks, and they simply could not draft enough water from the Patapsco River to overcome the fire's momentum.

Another serious fire struck Main Street less than a month later. On Saturday afternoon, October 8, 1977, a fire broke out at 8113 Main Street, in one of the oldest buildings in town. At the time, the building was occupied by the "You're Pictured" photography studio; the Prescetto family, part-owners of the studio, lived in an apartment above the studio. When she saw the thick black smoke pouring from the lower level of the building, Mrs. Prescetto gathered her two small children and leaned out of the front window and screamed for help. A passerby climbed the narrow ledge over the first

paid a very low weekly rent. At one point, the town housed as many as 750 workers. One longtime resident's earliest recollection of Alberton was when the blizzard of 1928 halted the response of the 1924 fire engine to an early morning fire Saturday, January 28, 1928.

On Wednesday, November 1, 1933, a fire destroyed eleven frame garages and eight automobiles owned by Alberton residents. Then, in the early 1940s, the mill, store, and all the housing was purchased by the C. R. Daniels Company. The name of the town, store, and post office were changed to Daniels in 1943. In the late 1960s, the C. R. Daniels Company decided they would not bring their mill town housing up to the recent enactment of the Howard County Rental Properties Housing Code.

The original buildings of the mill on the west side of the river dated back to the early nineteenth century. By the floor front door, took the children from Mrs. Prescetto, and handed them down to another bystander on the street. Mrs. Prescetto then climbed out through the window herself and made her way to safety. The interior of the building was almost completely destroyed by the flames, and the adjoining structure received smoke damage, but no one was injured.

That was the last major fire during the tenure of B. H. Shipley Jr. as chief of the Ellicott City Fire Department. On January 9, 1979, County Executive J. Hugh Nichols appointed Mr. Shipley to the position of Fire Administrator for Howard County. Since that post was now a full-time assignment, Chief Shipley regretfully tendered his resignation to the Ellicott City Volunteer Firemen's Association, which accepted it with an equal measure of regret and appreciation for his decades of service to the Company. Later that month, Executive Nichols also recommended Chief Shipley for the position of permanent Director of Civil Defense for Howard County.

On Saturday, March 3, 1979, the Ellicott City Volunteer Firemen's Association and the Ladies' Auxiliary joined to honor Mr. Shipley and his wife, Bessie, at a memorable banquet. Mr. Shipley did not, however, com-

pletely leave the Association. He was elected an emeritus member of the Board of Directors, as well as a life member of the Association's active department. In 1987, Mr. Shipley received yet another honor when he was elected to the Maryland State Firemen's Association Hall of Fame, thereby becoming part of the only father and son team to be placed in that distinguished group. At that time, Chief Shipley also received the coveted Marbery Gates Award, a prestigious honor given annually to outstanding firefighters who had garnered fifty or more years of service within their Department.

Clearly Mr. Shipley's boots would not be easy to fill. On January 25, 1979, the Board of Directors of the Ellicott City Volunteer Firemen's Association elected Captain Henry L. Long III as their new chief. Chief Long, however, remained in that office for only three years. On March 25, 1982, he offered his resignation, complaining that the

The 1984 six alarm Main Street fire.

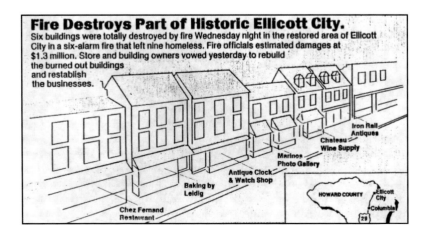

Fire Destroys Part of Historic Ellicott City.
Six buildings were totally destroyed by fire Wednesday night in the restored area of Ellicott City in a six-alarm fire that left nine homeless. Fire officials estimated damages at $1.3 million. Store and building owners vowed yesterday to rebuild the burned out buildings and restablish the businesses.

volunteer Board of Directors was interfering unduly in the operations of the Fire Department, and that morale among the career firefighters at the stations consequently was at its lowest point. "At the present time," Chief Long stated in his letter of resignation, "the Board has taken away all the authority of the Chief. Any member that has a complaint goes directly to the President [of the Association] for action. The President takes action with the advice of a Career Lieutenant concerning this information. The Chief is not contacted or advised."

The board subsequently voted to accept Long's resignation, replacing him with George E. Massey. Craig C. Proffen, president of the Association's Board of Directors, acknowledged that the Department had "definite morale problems among all personnel," but expressed his hope that a series of scheduled meetings and joint training sessions with both volunteer and career firefighters would alleviate the problem.

Such conflicts between volunteers and career firefighters were not limited to the Ellicott City Fire Department during the 1980s. Indeed, one of the major issues facing the Howard County fire companies in that decade was the integration of career staff and volunteer firefighters. As the number of volunteers continued to dwindle, most fire companies had to request the county to hire more career personnel. Nevertheless, county officials and Fire Department officers agreed that Howard County would need to rely on a joint volunteer-career firefighting force for the foreseeable future, since any move to establish an entirely paid, full-time firefighting force would impose a significant tax burden on county residents.

Career firefighters frequently found themselves in a dilemma at the scene of an emergency, when they received conflicting orders from a volunteer officer and a career officer of lower rank. To ameliorate the difficulties, Chief Massey attempted to enhance communication between the volunteer and paid personnel, and by June 1983, he was able to report that "there seem to be closer ties" between the two groups. In 1984, Chief Massey retired, and Deputy Chief John J. Klein assumed the post of chief of the Department.

On the evening of November 14, 1984, Ellicott City required all the firefighters it could muster when one of the worst fires in the history of the town began shortly after 11:00 P.M. in the back of Leidig's Bakery at 8149 Main Street. Flames flashed rapidly east to the Chez Ferdnand Restaurant at 8143 Main Street, and to the four wooden frame buildings immediately west of Leidig's: the Antique Clock and Watch Shop at 8149 Main Street, Marino's Photo Gallery at 8161 Main Street, Chateau Wine Supply at 8167 Main Street, and Iron Rail Antiques at 8167 Main Street. (Five of these buildings had suffered through the destructive fire of 1917; two had been completely rebuilt, and three others had required extensive repairs.) Although firefighters from the Main Street Station arrived less than a minute after receiving the first alarm, the fire had gained considerable momentum. According to one observer, the flames reached more than one hundred feet high at one point.

Recognizing that the fire could turn into a full-fledged inferno if it were not checked, firefighters concentrated on spraying long jets of water onto the two buildings at either end of the row to keep the fire from spreading further. As scores of residents and bystanders watched, the firefighters also directed streams of water onto the brick fronts of the buildings in the middle of the row to keep those structures from collapsing. Fortunately, the winds were not as high that night as they had been for the previous several days. Access to the rear of the buildings was hampered by the Tiber Branch, which ran parallel to Main Street at that point. To douse the flames that shot from the Iron Rail Shop, firemen had to work from the roof of the Ellicott City Rental Properties, the next building to the west.

Finally, after more than four hours, the firefighters brought the blaze under control, aided by the presence of the solid masonry walls of the Commercial and Farmers Bank at the east end of the stricken block, and the alley that separated Iron Rail Antiques from the Ellicott City Rental Properties building at the west end. All of the six buildings in between were completely ruined, however; estimates of the financial losses ran as high as $1.3 million. Nine people who lived in apartments above the stores were left homeless. "It's like a pain right in the heart," mourned one business owner. "We were flooded out in 1972 down the street," remembered another. "We lost everything, but we came back. We'll battle back again."

This time, however, the firefighters had not been hindered by a lack of water. They had stationed an engine to the rear of 3709 Old Columbia Pike, supplying hose lines across the Tiber Branch to the rear of the burning structures. The firefighters had also extended hose lines from a hydrant on St. Paul Street across the Tiber Branch to the rear of the buildings. A recent extension by Baltimore County of public water lines along Frederick Road to the Patapsco River Bridge gave the mutual aid Baltimore County Fire Department units the capability to connect to the hydrant near the river and lay a line to the fire scene. Thus Howard County's water system in the Ellicott City area, with new distribution and larger mains, supplied sufficient water to control the fire.

Although the November 14, 1984, fire was the worst conflagration in the history of Ellicott City, it was not the only major fire to strike the town during the 1980s. There already had been two serious fires in August 1982. One damaged a section of the Court House Square Office Complex, which was under construction at 3565 Ellicott Mills Drive, and another destroyed the former Ellicott City Elementary School at 3700 College Avenue. The latter blaze sent flames reaching so high into the sky that, as one observer put it, "It looked like the sun coming up, but in the west, in the wrong direction." Investigators suspected that both of these fires were deliberately set by one or more arsonists.

On March 16, 1986, yet another fire struck the Wilkins-Rogers mill on the east side of the Patapsco River. Although this blaze was not quite as destructive as the 1941 fire that had gutted so many buildings of the Doughnut Corporation of America on the same site, it grew to a five-alarm conflagration that involved almost one hundred firefighters and caused approximately $1.5 million worth of damage. The atmosphere surrounding the fire became extremely tense when it was discovered that a gas main that ran through the room in which the fire started had not yet been shut off, which naturally created the fear of an explosion. "If the walls did not fall down on the firefighters," noted a Baltimore County fire official, "they feared the gas main would explode or the floor would collapse." Through the use of high expansion foam, the firefighters managed to bring the fire under control seven and one half hours after the first alarm was called in.

Another series of deliberately set fires occurred in Ellicott City between July 26 and November 21, 1987. All nine of these fires were set in buildings in the 8400 block of Frederick Road. As the fires followed one another throughout the late summer and early autumn, local residents grew extremely apprehensive. "People are concerned that a fire would spread through the frame row houses and someone inside will die or a firefighter will get hurt," explained one

Main Street businessman. Fortunately, police apprehended a local resident and charged him with setting three of the fires. At the end of November 1987, one more suspicious fire occurred in a vacant apartment near the scene of the previous nine fires, in an apartment complex that was scheduled to be rented to low and moderate income tenants, but investigators concluded that it probably had been set by someone else.

Less than a year later, another suspicious fire occurred in a townhouse development that was under construction in the 8600 block of Manahan Drive. Four townhouses—each almost half-completed—were completely destroyed. As if the town had not suffered enough from arson, a fire that broke out on January 22, 1989, in the basement of the Main Street Magic Emporium, at 8181 Main Street, also was charged to the work of one or more arsonists.

Perhaps the most disheartening case of arson occurred Friday, January 5, 1990, when fire swept through the grounds of the thirty-two-acre Enchanted Forest Amusement Park on 10500 Baltimore National Pike. Opened in 1955, the gentle attractions of the Enchanted Forest, with their fairy tale themes, had entertained thousands of young children over the years. Its original owners had sold the park to a devel-

opment group less than twelve months earlier, and the new owners were planning to use part of the property for the construction of a shopping center. The fire destroyed most of the two-story building known as Robin Hood's Barn, which housed the park's snack bar and gift shop. Police subsequently arrested three Baltimore County teenagers and charged them with trespassing, theft, and malicious burning. "The fire," concluded a spokesman for the Fire Marshal, "was more of an afterthought once they were in the building."

But the most spectacular fires of the early 1990s took place on historic Main Street. In February and March 1992, a series of deliberately set blazes caused significant property damage to a number of Ellicott City commercial establishments, and created a climate of intense apprehension among local residents and businessmen. Just before midnight on the evening of February 19, 1992, flames broke out in the Ellicott City Country Store at 8190 Main

The Firehouse Museum, 3829 Church Road. Dedication September 21, 1991. Sixty-eight years elapsed between the time the local fire company moved out and the building was restored to its original 1889 design.

Street, which already had suffered from a previous fire in May 1972. Although firefighters were hindered by the steep hills, narrow pathways, and rock abutments behind the building, their aggressive attack managed to restrict the fire to the Country Store and its immediate neighbor to the west, the Heirlooms Too Antique Shop.

Several weeks later, an even worse blaze began when an arsonist started a fire in the basement of the warehouse of Taylor's Furniture of Ellicott City, at 8301 Hamilton Street, directly behind the U.S. Post Office. The warehouse building, which dated back to the 1880s, originally had been used as a stable; successive owners had turned it into a machine shop and a car dealership, before Taylor's Furniture purchased it. Again, Ellicott City's unique topography created difficulties for the firefighters, as the Tiber Branch—which ran right under the warehouse—prevented them from moving their equipment close to the fire. To keep the blaze from spreading to the nearby shops on Tongue Row, firefighters kept a constant stream of water playing on the buildings. By the time the one-hundred-foot high flames finally died down, the entire warehouse and its contents had been completely destroyed.

By this time, Ellicott City merchants were growing quite nervous. "Basically, it's going to be, 'How do we stop fires in Ellicott City?" asked the president of the town's Business Association. "We're definitely very concerned about the fires around here," noted another longtime businesswoman. "It gives you a very uneasy feeling." Their fears were not assuaged when another fire broke out March 8, although this time the damage to a vacant building in the 8400 block of Frederick Road was relatively minor.

Police stepped up their patrols of the area, and Fire Department officials met with business leaders to offer their suggestions on fire awareness and prevention. At last their vigilance paid off, and a suspect was arrested March 12 as he attempted to start another fire in a shop on Maryland Avenue. The alleged arsonist, a thirty-three-year-old pharmacist who lived in Catonsville, was subsequently charged with setting a string of fires in Ellicott City and Columbia. When he explained to a trial judge that he had heard voices telling him to set the fires, the judge ruled that he was not criminally responsible by reason of insanity and confined him to a hospital in Jessup until authorities determine that he was no longer a danger to himself or to society.

In the midst of this unprecedented

series of deliberately set fires, the Ellicott City Volunteer Firemen's Association continued to expand its efforts to educate the public on fire prevention and safety. Each year, during Fire Prevention Week in early October, the Association held open houses at Fire Station No. 2 and No. 8, sponsored "Fire Safety Days" at several shopping malls, demonstrated fire safety techniques to children and adults, and visited local schools with its equipment and educational literature.

To further enhance the community's understanding of the role firefighters have played in the history of Ellicott City and the Howard County Fire Department, the Firehouse Museum at 3829 Church Road was officially opened September 21, 1991. The idea of turning the original site of Fire Company No. 1's engine house into a museum had first been broached by the Ellicott City Volunteer Firemen's Association in 1967, and the Association had formally voted in January 1972 in favor of restoring the building to a fire museum. By January 1989, the Howard County government had decided to take an active role in the restoration project, which it viewed as "an exciting project" and "a unique partnership" between the government and private organizations, including the

Volunteer Firemen's Association.

Over the years, the site of the museum had served a wide variety of purposes. It had originally been donated to the Fire Company No. 1 by Christian Eckert as a site for a firehouse. First occupied in August 1889, when the firehouse building was still a shell, the property had been conveyed to the city government in 1907. For the next several decades, it had been used both to house firefighting equipment and for various other municipal purposes. Occasionally drunks were locked in the firehouse by the town policeman to "sleep it off." When the new firehouse opened in 1924, the Fire Company had no use for the building, but the city continued to use it for its own purposes.

From 1924 to 1935, the site served as a garage for the town's Model T Ford dump truck. In July 1935, the land and building were conveyed to the Howard County Board of County Commissioners, and the county's welfare office occupied the building from August 1935 to March 1962. In April 1962, the Howard County Environmental Health Office took up residence there, remaining until June 1967. For the next two years, the building was vacant. It was supposed to house a branch of the

Looking northeast from 3774 Old Columbia Pike, a sketch shows Old Columbia Pike and Howard County Court House hill.

Howard County Public Library, but the County Commissioners withheld the necessary funding until the winter of 1969. In March 1969, the library branch finally opened, and remained at that location until November 1988. Over the next year and a half, numerous groups—including the Howard County Employment and Training Center, and the Home Builders Association of Maryland—contributed their talents and labor to the restoration of the building, with a view toward turning it into a fire museum.

When the museum opened to the public September 21, 1991, visitors could view a fascinating display of firefighting equipment from the town's past, including the 1892 two-wheeled hose cart, the Baltimore & Ohio Railroad's bell that served as the community's fire alarm from 1894 to 1896, the "Big Bell" that subsequently became the fire alarm for more than forty years, an assortment of turnout gear and hand-held apparatus from previous decades as well as a section of the sliding brass pole that stood at the fire station (8390 Main Street) from 1939 to 1984. A question was asked by a young teenager while visiting the Firehouse Museum as to when the first brass firehouse pole was put into use. This question could not be answered at that time. Further inquiry revealed that in the mid-1800s

the Fire Patrol of New York City began using brass poles so their men could slide down from their second floor bunk room to the wagon bay. The primary purpose of the Fire Patrol unit was to remove and protect the contents of a burning building

The Association also paused to honor its past in July 1988, when it celebrated its one hundredth anniversary with a gala dinner that featured a keynote speech from former Chief B. H. Shipley Jr., a resolution of gratitude and congratulations from the County Council, a trophy awarded to the Association by the local post of the Veterans of Foreign Wars, and a message of congratulations from President Ronald Reagan. "You have always responded to the call for help from neighbors and friends, placing their safety and well-being above your own," wrote President Reagan. "Because of the dedication of individuals like you, America is a better place in which to live."

Throughout its history, the Ellicott City Volunteer Firemen's Association has always enjoyed a measure of stability among its leadership from one generation to the next, largely due to the involvement of entire families in the work of the Association. Such was the case with Chief John J. Klein, a successful local businessman who assumed the position of chief in 1984 after twenty-five years of service as a volunteer fire-fighter. Numerous members of Chief Klein's family had been involved in the work of the Association and the Ladies' Auxiliary, including both his parents, two sisters, three brothers, and his two children. Moreover, his wife, Carolyn, is a volunteer who also serves on the Board of Directors of the Association. "It's something that runs in the blood—a desire to help someone," Chief Klein once explained. "It's not a lifetime job, but I enjoy helping people. That's what it's all about."

Under Chief Klein's leadership, the Ellicott City Fire Department is planning to move out of their Main Street Station into a new building on a two-acre site at the intersection of Montgomery Road and Old Columbia Pike. From their new home—which will include eight apparatus bays, sleeping quarters for career and volunteer personnel, and a physical training room—the firefighters will be able to respond more quickly to fires outside of downtown Ellicott City. The new station will also include special quarters to house the Association's Engine No. 1, the American LaFrance pumper which the Volunteer Fire Company put into service December 27, 1929. The Company retired Engine No. 1 in October 1961. The engine was subsequently owned by several different individuals. In June 1992, the Ellicott City Volunteer Firemen's Association repurchased the engine and, with the help of local craftsmen, restored it to its original condition.

Although more than a century of improvements have transformed the science of fighting fires, the commitment required of firefighters—whether career or volunteer—has not changed. The membership of the Ellicott City Volunteer Firemen's Association has expanded, both in terms of numbers and in the range of applicants accepted. All members of the Department are considered as equals and are eligible to serve in any capacity within the Department. But they all must maintain the traditions that began with the founding of Engine Company No. 1 in 1888:

SERVICE — ANYWHERE— ANYTIME

INDEX

A

Abel, Vernon T.   193
Alberton Mills 94, 194
Ambulance, First   165, 166
Angelo Cottage   73
Ash, Charles E.   156

B

Bells:
   1894 - B & O Locomotive   17
   1896 - J. Register "Big Bell"   18, 67
Bethany Fire Station No. 8   189
Biggs, Robert 58
Bloom, Henry E.   54
Bossom, E. Reid   157
Brandenburg, Donald L.   99, 102
Brian, Thomas E.   113
Brust, Mildred A.   144
Brown, Dr. Louis L.   79, 119, 122
Buetefisch, Charles E.   67, 80, 92, 97
Burgess, Samuel F.   84, 86

C

Caplan, Altra 30
Carr, George W.   83, 92, 113, 132
Carnival, First 68
Cavey, Elmer C.   69, 92, 113
Chenoweth's Boarding School for Girls   91
Churches:
   Emory M. E.   76, 77, 96
   First Baptist of Ellicott City   77
   First Lutheran 76
   First Presbyterian 76, 77
   Mt. Zion A.M.E. 77
   St. Lukes A.M.E. 77
   St. Paul's Catholic 36, 76, 123
   St. Peter's Episcopal 60, 76, 130
C & P Telephone Co.   25
Citizen Telephone Co.   25
Clark:

Edward T.   78, 180
E. T. Jr. 189
Judge James   90, 92, 96
Senator James Jr.   176
J. Booker   43, 52, 53, 55, 69
J. Lawrence   59
Louis T.   91
Collette:
   Frank K.   66, 113
   Thomas W.   146, 169
   William F.   146
Communications   143, 162-164, 173, 179
Court House   24, 28, 115, 180
Courts, Howard B.   69
Covered Wooden Bridge   28, 34, 38
Cullum:
   Elmer M. Jr.   153
   George M.   153, 190
Cumberland, Charles   82, 83

D

Dalton Farm   59
Daniels, C. R.   191, 193, 194
Delosier:
   C. E.   71, 94, 102
   C. E. Jr.   163, 168, 169, 174, 190
Dickey Mills   50, 54, 126
Ditch, Charles P.   108, 113, 146, 156, 159
Dorsey, Col. Charles W.   15
Doughnut Corp. Of America   125, 135-137
Dundee Summer Hotel   91

E

Easton:
   Clinton M.   141
   Milton H.   54, 55, 57, 62
Easton Funeral Home   165, 180
Easton Sons' Hall   29
Eckert, Christian 11, 12, 84
Elk-Ridge Farm   52, 53, 55, 58

Elkridge Volunteer Fire Co.   142
Ellicott City Lions Club   191
Ellicott City Rotary Club   96, 101
Ellicott City Times 28, 42, 57, 61, 71, 79, 103, 109,
    124, 127, 131, 135
Ellicott's Country Store   110, 187, 200
Emory M. E. Church   76, 77, 96
Engines:
    First Horse Drawn   16, 17
    First Motorized   62, 63, 65
Elysville Cotton Mill 193
Eslin, James F.   167

F
Feigley, Richard S.   43, 46, 47, 51, 52, 84
Fifth District Volunteer Fire Dept. 146
Fire Dog:
    Yogi 191-193
    JR 193
Fires, Main Street   14, 19, 20, 24, 25, 35, 39, 41, 51-
    53, 59, 130, 131, 140, 141, 175, 186, 187, 194,
    195, 199, 200
Firehouses:
    First   12
    Second   64, 93
    Third   125, 126
    Fourth   44, 45
Firehouse Museum 65, 199, 201
Fire Plug 21
First Baptist Church of Ellicott City   77
First Fire Hydrant   21
First Lutheran Church 76
First Presbyterian Church 76, 77
Forty Acres   122, 123
Fuller, Joseph M.   184

G
Gaither:
    James Jr.   24, 43
    Thomas M.   61

Gaither, James H. Livery Stable   9, 18, 21, 24, 25,
    127
Gambrill, C. A. Mfg. Co.   8, 48, 49, 54
Gambrill, Dr. William B.   43, 59, 85
German Evangelical Lutheran Church   27
Glenwood Institute   71
Green Cross Garage   65, 68, 81, 85, 86
Greenwood, Albert   69, 102, 103
Grimes:
    H. Thomas   92
    Thaddeus   107

H
Hansen, Dr. George B.   167
Hebb, William S.   99, 102, 103
Heine, Frank   11, 12, 19
Helm, G. Ray   66, 90, 92, 102
Hermann, Charles A.   26, 38, 58, 83
Hewett, Daniel D.   76
Higinbothom:
    Dulany C.   43
    F. C.   84, 132, 165, 166
    Justice Frank C.   82, 83, 105
Hillsinger:
    J. W.   112
    Loretta J.   112
    Stephan   85
Hilton, Edward D.   21, 93
Hodges:
    Addison   69
    William S.   69
Holtman, Bessie   25
Hood, Robert E.   113
Hoplites   123
Hose Reel   17
Howard County Jail   82, 83
Howard County Police   75, 124, 175
Howard House   28, 84, 143
Howard Telephone Co.   25
Hubbel, Charles   104, 105

Hunt, Nathan 69
Hurricanes:
    Agnes 187, 188, 191, 194
    Eliose 40, 191
Hyatt, Sydney J. 69

I
Ilchester 39, 99, 111

J
Jacob, William F. 155
Johnson:
    Dr. J. Hartley 43, 52
    Nimrod 35
Jones, Omar J. 185, 186

K
Kerger, Joseph 51
Kinlein, Julius A. 92
Kinsel, L. J. 12
Kirkwood:
    John C. 110
    William F. 22, 92
    William F. Jr. 146
Klein:
    Charles A. 146, 158
    Edward 158
    John J. 190, 196, 203
    William F. 170
Kraft, Mayor John H. 42
Kraft Meat Market 22, 78, 151
Kramer, J. H. 30, 78
Kroh, Mayor J. Edwin 43, 90, 91, 102, 103, 127

L
Ladies Auxiliary 114-116, 126, 129, 143, 149, 190
Laumann:
    Albert H. 110
    John 69
    Philip 78, 79
Leishear, Mayor Joseph H. Jr. 22
Liburn 64
Ligon, Mary T. 15
Lilly:
    Thomas 69
    William F. 80, 82
Lisbon Volunteer Fire Co. 142, 147
Long, Henry L. III 190, 195, 196
Loughran, John 51, 79
Lyons, John H. 69, 102

M
McCauley, W. T. 11, 18
McCubbins Ice Pond 146, 154
McNabb:
    Edward S. 66
    Leonard A. 66, 71

Maginnis, John C. 61, 64
Makinson:
    Charles T. 30, 35, 47
    H. O. 66, 69, 99, 102
    Mary Rebecca 122
Martin:
    Andrew 81
    Dr. Isaac Jr. 25
Maryland Telephone Co. 25
Massey:
    Charles A. 156, 190
    George E. 167, 190, 196
    Howard J. Jr. 153
    Howard J. III 190
Maupinis University School 13
Mayfield:
    Thomas Hunt 71
    T. H. Jr. 69, 71, 127
    William F. 11, 43, 80
Meldron, J. Raymond 69
Mellor:
    Benjamin 11-13, 16, 18
    Benjamin Jr. 43, 62, 63, 69, 71, 90, 92, 94, 96,
        97, 113, 146, 149, 190
Mercier, Owen H. 11, 18
Merson, Thomas F. 190
Miller:
    Charles E. 65, 81, 146, 149
    Edwin A. 113
    Dr. Frank O. 85
    Henry L. 146
    Preston P. 66, 69, 71
Miller Chevrolet Sales 64, 155
Mt. Misery Lane 27
Mt. Zion A.M.E. Church 77
Mullineaux, Lester 69
Mullinix, Thomas 153
N
New Assembly Room 13
Noll:
    Adam 69
    Hart B. 91
Norris, Mayor Edward 15

O
O'Kisco Flouring Mill 193
Oldfield, Hamilton 20, 85
Oppenheim Oberdorf Co. 28
Otten, Francis J. Jr. 110

P
Parks, Albert 69
Patapsco Flouring Mills 8, 47-49
Patapsco Heights 106, 107
Patapsco Hotel 32
Patapsco Manor Sanitorium 61, 62, 109
Patapsco National Bank 51, 61, 63, 76, 82, 96, 151

Penny, H. Grafton   127
Pfeiffer, William Jr.   190
Pindell, Antoinette   111
Post Office:
    Columbia   54
    Ellicott City   127-129
Powell, Col. William S.   27
Proffen, Craig C.   196

R

Radcliffe's Emporium   23, 39, 180
Renewal, Urban   180, 181
Richards, Frederick A.   170
Ridgely, Judge Robert H.   15
Rock Hill College   56, 59-61, 91, 122
Rodey, Edward A.   65, 66, 68, 69, 82
Rodgers, Cabel D.   54, 91
Route 40   125, 133
Ruth, Herman "Babe"   122, 123
Ryan, Rev. Michael A.   60, 61

S

Savage Volunteer Fire Co.   123
Scaggs, Bradley T.   18
Schools:
    Ellicott City Black Elementary   75
    Ellicott City Elementary & High   16, 20, 22, 26,
        27, 74, 75
    German Evangelical Luthern Church   27
    Hill Street   27, 28
    Old Friends Meeting House   27
    St. Paul's Black Parochial   76
    St. Paul's Parochial   75
    St. Paul the Apostle   76
    Resurrection/St. Paul   76
Schone, Mae R.   144
Scott, Melville   86, 131
Shipley:
    B. Harrison   65, 69, 105, 111, 113, 114, 117, 119-
        121, 127-129, 134, 143, 149, 157, 166, 184,
        185
    B. Harrison Jr.   60, 67, 77, 90, 92, 102, 110, 119,
        152, 162, 166, 169, 174, 179, 183, 185,
        186, 190, 195, 202
    Frank M.   10
    Georgia   105
    Mary J. (May)   90, 115, 149
    Robert T.   105, 106
Shreeve, Dr. James E.   57, 84
Sirens, Traffic   117
Starr, Scott M.   84
Steward, James   56, 79
Stigler, Joseph P.   156, 160
St. Charles College   33, 34
St. Luke's A.M.E. Church 77
St. Paul's Catholic Church   36, 76, 123
St. Peter's Episcopal Church   60, 76, 130
Stromberg, Paul J.   127

T

Talbott:
    Edward W.   92, 112
    George Alexander   21, 84, 97
    Richard   43, 66
    Sara Rebecca   21, 101
    Thomas M.   97
Talbott & Clark's Lumber Yard   15
Talbott Lumber Co.   46, 47, 64, 93
Tarro, Rev. Peter B.   36
Taylor:
    Isaac H.   42, 43
    Lloyd G.   157, 167
Taylor Manor Hospital   61, 186
Teal, William   74
Telephones, Emergency   179
Thompson, Carl   69
Tittsworth, W. Vernon   102, 103
Tongue Row   141, 172
Trolleys   19, 21-23, 34, 35, 37, 38, 61, 84, 88, 144,
    145
Trollinger, Martha A.   184

W

Walker-Chandler House   186, 187
Wallenhorst:
    Justice B. H.   11, 14, 29
    Charles B.   39, 46, 62
    C. Edwin   110
Wamsley, L. Burgess   69, 99, 102, 103
Warfield:
    Edward S.   85, 86
    Governor Edwin   28
Werner, Mayor Charles J.   10
West Friendship Volunteer Fire Dept.   142, 147
Westphall, Herman   104, 105
White Hall   15
White, Dr. W. Rushmere   62
Wilson, Robert C.   18
Wosch, Julius   30, 34, 43, 59, 95, 105

Y

Yates:
    Charles   82
    Harrison   69
    Robert G.   85, 87
    Samuel J.   22, 80, 127

ABOUT THE AUTHOR

All of B. H. Shipley Jr.'s life has been spent in Ellicott City. He continues to live there with his wife, Bessie. Many people have come to recognize him as an expert in the history of the town. Early childhood memories include playing along Main Street and the surrounding hills of Ellicott City. Currently, Mr. Shipley serves as a director with the Howard County Historical Society.

Mr. Shipley was born and raised in a fire service family. He continued this tradition by serving the Ellicott City Volunteer Firemen's Association, Inc. for forty-nine years. Upon his retirement as a volunteer, Mr. Shipley accepted the position of fire administrator for Howard County. He is a life member of the Active Department and emeritus member of the Board of Directors of the Ellicott City Volunteer Firemen's Association, Inc. He served as the department chief for twenty years. His service continues as the historian for the organization.